Praise for *Hit the Deck*

"*Hit the Deck* shows founders what they *really* need to know in order to plan and pitch their startup ideas effectively. It explains the rules of thumb followed by sophisticated investors and experienced entrepreneurs, in an easy-to-follow, no-nonsense way."

~ Owen Davis, Managing Director, NYCSeed.

"A street-smart guide to raising money for startups. It shows entrepreneurs how to create plans that communicate critical aspects of their business, and how to engage investors in conversations."

~ William Sahlman, professor of entrepreneurship and Associate Dean at Harvard Business School.

"A great book for entrepreneurs looking to turn ideas into businesses. I particularly like the way you walk readers through an actual investor pitch, slide by slide. Your advice is right on target, your writing is clear and easy to follow, and you've peppered the book with practical advice and examples from real-world startups".

~ Andrew Macey, member of Common Angels, Global Board member, MIT Enterprise Forum, and VP Digital Strategy, Sapient.

"An excellent book! Very much in keeping with my own sentiments about business plans. One of the key takeaways is that business plans are living documents. If your plan is not evolving, your company is not evolving."

~ James Robinson IV, Co-founder and Managing Partner of RRE Ventures.

"Startups win by being fast and flexible. That goes for planning, as well as execution. This book helps founders plan just enough to make smart choices, without wasting time and effort."

~ Amar Bhide, former professor of entrepreneurship at Columbia Business School, Harvard Business School, and University of Chicago's Graduate School of Business.

"Just the kind of book first-time entrepreneurs need. It provides invaluable tools, with a practical, hands-on approach, including a thorough pre-launch checklist. I wish I had this tool while I was teaching."

~ John W. Altman, former professor of entrepreneurship at The University of California, Berkeley, and VP of Strategic Futures for the Kauffman Center for Entrepreneurial Leadership.

"There's at least one piece of wisdom on every page of Hit The Deck, none of it buried in jargon."

~ Barrett Hazeltine, professor and former Associate Dean, Brown University.

"Great advice for entrepreneurs! Your approach forces founders to communicate their ideas clearly."

~ Michael Roberts, Executive Director, Arthur Rock Center for Entrepreneurship at the Harvard Business School.

"Hit The Deck does a superb job of explaining what matters for modern business plans and pitch decks. Angel investors and venture capitalists everywhere will be thankful if entrepreneurs read this book and take it to heart."

~ David Cohen, Founder and CEO, Techstars.

HIT THE DECK

create a business plan in half the time with twice the impact

Includes:

- *Step-by-step guide to creating a business plan presentation*
- *Advice and insights from entrepreneurs and investors*
- *Sample business plans, presentations and pitches*

David Ronick

Published by UpStart Bootcamp, LLC.

Copyright © 2010 by David Ronick

ISBN: 978-0-9827402-0-0

Contents

Acknowledgements

Thanks to all the people who helped with the book and the thinking that led up to it, including:

- John W. Altman
- Gabrielle Bernstein
- Amar Bhide
- Casey Boyle
- Steve Brotman
- Sara Clemence
- David Cohen
- Frances Cole Jones
- Owen Davis
- Susan Debbie
- Chip Hazard
- Barrett Hazeltine
- Allison Hemming
- Tommy Hilfiger
- Jennifer Houser
- Susan Kittenplan
- Mo Koyfman
- Scott Kraft
- Liz Lange
- Dany Levy
- Andrew Macey
- Lee Newman
- Bo Peabody
- Ronnie Peters
- Michael Roberts
- James Robinson IV
- Jenene Ronick
- Ted Ronick
- William Sahlman
- Ted Schlein
- Margot Schupf
- Jinal Shah
- Amanda Steinberg
- Leanne Taylor
- Joe Watson

Dedication

This book is dedicated to:

- My wife Jenene, a naturally gifted entrepreneur and constant source of inspiration

- Our son Jackson, my most rewarding startup

- My father Ted, whose generosity, support, and loyalty never cease to amaze me

- My mother Beverly, my angel investor

- Susan, my sister—always there for me in good times and bad

- My clients and students—fellow entrepreneurs out there making it happen every day

- Jenn, my partner, who makes me a better entrepreneur every day

Introduction

There are hundreds of books on business planning. Why read this one?

- Hit the Deck isn't just a book; it's part of something bigger: UpStart Bootcamp (upstartbootcamp.com)—an online school for entrepreneurs. Having bought the book, you're entitled to 10% off your first purchase. For more information, visit upstartbootcamp.com/promo.

- The book and the site are part of something even *bigger*: A new approach to planning and launching startups. Today's entrepreneurs get more results in less time, with less money. They follow a new set of best practices, honed in places most entrepreneurs never see, like the offices of venture capital firms in Silicon Valley. UpStart is leveling the playing field, making these methods accessible to a broader audience.

- Business plans have changed along with startups. A decade ago, a business plan looked like a college term paper—40+ pages of written prose, with footnotes, charts, and appendices. Developing that type of plan took months. Today, planning a business happens much faster. Entrepreneurs don't waste time writing term papers nobody reads. Instead, business plans take the form of short, compelling presentations—aka "decks"—that are pitched in-person. Using slides instead of prose takes half the time and has twice the impact on potential investors and other audiences.

- In this book, you'll learn about the *right* way to plan new companies. I'll explain how it's done, step by step. You'll also hear from successful investors and entrepreneurs, who share their experience and advice in interviews throughout the book.

Part One:
The Business Planning Process

If you are starting a business, you should develop a business plan. But as an entrepreneurial spirit, you probably don't like to be told what to do—at least not without knowing "what" and "why." This part of the book will answer those questions, including:

- Do I *really* need a business plan? Why?
- What exactly *is* a business plan?
- How long will it take to develop a business plan?

CHAPTER 1

You Need a Business Plan (Yes, This Means You)

Here's why a business plan can help you:

- Starting a business tends to be an emotional experience and it's easy to lose sight of the facts. Business planning helps you take an objective look at your strategy and your approach to make sure you've considered the most important issues, including the economics of the business and how you'll get rewarded for all of your hard work in the end.

- If you have business partners, a plan ensures that all of you are on the same page. That goes for family and life partners, too. If you're married, for example, a business plan can help you get your spouse on board. As you go through the emotional and financial ups and downs of building a company, you'll need all the support you can get on the home front.

- You can't do this alone. You'll need to run your ideas by others, such as members of your advisory board or experts in your industry, to get advice and feedback,. A good business plan makes that easy.

- If you want to raise capital for a business, you'll want to communicate your vision to investors in a persuasive, compelling way. A good business plan will help you do just that. In fact, a study by Babson College found that startups with a business plan raised twice as much capital as those without a business plan within their first 12 months.[1]

Of course, it's never too late to write—or update—a business plan. Many of my clients have run their company for years before reaching out to me. Some want to make sure they're on the right track. Others want to change course or raise capital.

---

1   Pre-Startup Formal Business Plans and Post-Startup Performance: A Study of 116 New Ventures, *Venture Capital Journal,* Vol. 9, No. 4, pp. 1-20, October 2007 .

Ask the Expert

Steve Brotman: "A business without a plan is like a boat without a rudder."

Steve Brotman is a Managing Director of Greenhill & Co., and co-founder and co-head of Greenhill SAVP, a fund that invests in early-stage technology and information services companies. Steve currently sits on the board of four companies and the MIT Enterprise Forum's New York chapter. Steve founded AdOne Classified Network, one of the nation's leading classified ad Web sites, which was acquired by Hearst, Scripps, and Advance-Newhouse. Steve is a graduate of Duke University and has a joint JD/MBA from Washington University.

UpStart: "In what ways do you think it benefits a startup team to go through the process of developing a business plan?"

Steve Brotman: "A business without a plan is like a boat without a rudder. You've got to have a plan! Developing that plan is the critical first step of business creation. It commits you and your team to an explicit strategy and approach. It ensures that your founding team is aligned behind common goals. It defines both what you will do, and what you won't do. And it establishes priorities, so startups focus time and resources on what's most critical for their success. Finally, it allows founders to communicate their vision to investors, advisors, employees, vendors and partners. That doesn't mean the plan can't or won't change. So be flexible, and when a major change needs to happen, circle the wagons, and put together a new plan."

UpStart: "Would you ever invest in a company without a business plan?"

Steve Brotman: "It's doubtful. In the earliest stages of a company, founders start with the equivalent of an idea on the back of a napkin. But every startup needs help, even if that's just from the landlord and lawyer. Getting that help demands more than just what's on the napkin—it requires a business plan. That said, some entrepreneurs go overboard on their plans and projections, and prefer to write about their plans versus doing something about them. That's not what a plan is about. The goal is uniting your team behind some shared vision and objectives, and how you will likely meet those objectives, and having some document to show parties you'd like to bring on board that will increase the likelihood of your venture's success."

What's the risk of not developing a business plan? Consider this cautionary tale about an entrepreneur I'll call "Deborah." When I met Deborah, her corporate events business was booming. With just one assistant and a sublet office, she was generating $250,000 in annual sales. As more clients signed on, she hired several more employees and moved into a new office.

But then things started to unwind. She lost interest in executing the events and wanted to focus on selling. Then her biggest account filed Chapter 11 and she found herself in a cash crunch.

Deborah hadn't hired key lieutenants, so she had to do all the management work herself. She thought about selling the business, but hadn't developed an exit strategy. In the end, Deborah shut down her business with very little to show for it.

Next time, she'll write a business plan.

Takeaways

- If you are starting a business, large or small, you need a business plan.
- Developing a plan makes your goals and vision explicit. That's important for you as well as for your team if you have one. That's also important because you're going to need help, and the plan will let you communicate your approach to outsiders, including advisors, potential partners and employees, suppliers, and investors.

Learn more at upstartbootcamp.com

CHAPTER 2

What a Business Plan Is (And Isn't)

When I started helping entrepreneurs plan new companies, I discovered something curious—there was a lot of confusion about what, exactly, a business plan should look like. A business plan was once a lengthy, prose-based document written with word processing software like Microsoft Word, similar to a 40+ page college term paper. Sophisticated entrepreneurs and investors moved away from that format, but the typical entrepreneur on Main Street didn't get the message.[2] That's no surprise, since many books on business plans still recommended a term-paper-style business plan. Were the books simply out of date?

To make sure, I decided to ask the experts. I surveyed over 50 people, including venture capitalists (VCs) from leading firms like Kleiner, Perkins, Caufield & Byers, noted angel investors such as the backers of Method and serial entrepreneurs like John Osher, creator of the Crest SpinBrush. The results: 95 percent recommend

---

2   There are exceptions, such as requirements from some lending organizations like banks or the SBA, but they typically lend to companies with at least three years of operating history, not to startups.

that startups use a presentation format, not a term-paper-style plan.[3, 4] Here's why the pitch deck has taken the place of the text document:

1   A term-paper-style business plan takes too long to read. In this age of rampant Attention Deficit Disorder and communications overload, asking someone to read a 40+ page paper is pushing it. Why burden someone whose help you are seeking? And why take the risk that your plan won't be read at all?

2. A term-paper-style plan takes too long to write and update. Writing 40+ pages of prose takes months. Plus, a business plan isn't a static document—startups modify their plan continuously. Updating a page or chapter of text can take hours. Updating a bullet point or graphic in a slide presentation takes minutes.

3. Pitching in person is far more persuasive than sending a document for people to read. A deck is made for presentations, while a term paper is about as useful in a pitch as a doorstop. When you deliver a presentation in person, you can see how people are reacting, modify your pitch on the fly, address concerns or confusion immediately, and get feedback.

4. Presentations force startups to set priorities. If you are working with a 40-page plan, you can drop in every great idea that comes to mind. But when it comes time to explaining your ideas—and to executing those ideas—you'll have to focus. Culling your ideas down to those worthy of inclusion in a short presentation is a great way to start prioritizing.

---

3   Most of the others said they like to see a two- to four-page executive summary.

4   Thoughout this book we'll refer to presentations using terms including "pitch" and "deck" and "pitch deck." In some cases the individual pages of a presentation will be called "slides." In general, presentations are documents created with software like Microsoft PowerPoint or Apple Keynote, designed to facilitate in-person pitches.

So, what does a pitch deck look like? It's generally comprised of about 15 slides, each with just a few images and words. As we'll see, a great deck is typically minimalist in nature—clean and simple. The slides in your deck will serve as a roadmap for your presentation, but the most important points will come from your mouth, not from words on slides.

One of the best books on business planning is Guy Kawasaki's *The Art of the Start*. Here are a few of Kawasaki's points that I find particularly useful:

- "The gist of pitching is to get off to a fast start, explain the relevance of what you do, stay at a high level, listen to audience reaction, and then pitch over and over until you get it right."

- "Explain yourself (and what your company will do) in the first minute of your pitch (e.g. we sell software / fashion accessories / juice, etc.)."

- "Keep your pitch to 20 minutes ... I've never heard a pitch that was too short."

Later in the book, I'll show you how to develop a great pitch deck, slide-by-slide. I'll also describe supporting materials you'll need, like a one-page synopsis.

But first, there's one other key document you'll need to develop in tandem with your business plan deck—your financial model. A financial model is a set of financial projections built in Excel. The financial model should include a projection of profit and loss (also called a "P&L" or "Income Statement") for five years. If your cash cycle is fairly neutral, such as if you get paid immediately upon closing a sale (e.g., by credit card), you can probably get by with just the P&L. If on the other hand, you anticipate having a gap between when you pay expenses and get paid by customers, you should build a balance sheet and statement of cash flow.

For the sake of time, don't open the Excel spreadsheet during your business plan pitch meetings. Instead, cut and paste a few charts from your model into your slide presentation. In addition, explain to your audience that you've built a full financial model, including a set of assumptions, and that you'll be happy to share the full spreadsheet with them as you get further down the path (e.g., if an investor expresses serious interest in writing you a check).

We'll cover financial projections in more depth later in the book.

 # Food for Thought

Sequoia Capital is the venture capital firm that backed Google, Yahoo, YouTube, eHarmony, LinkedIn, and PayPal, among many other winners. On their Web site (www.sequoiacap.com), they offer the following advice:

"We like business plans that present a lot of information in as few words as possible … 15-20 slides … is all that's needed."

New York Angels is one of the leading groups of angel investors in the U.S. They've invested over $20 million in 65 early-stage, New York-area technology and new media companies. At www.newyorkangels.com, you'll see the following suggestions about the format of business plans:

"Slideshows with under 20 slides are generally most effective … Use the limited time you have for your presentation to emphasize the compelling factors about your investment opportunity and save unnecessary technology details for future meetings…"

More resources:

The Art of the Start: The Time-Tested, Battle-Hardened Guide for Anyone Starting Anything, by Guy Kawasaki. Kawasaki is a venture capitalist and was the "evangelist" for Apple's Macintosh computer. In this book, Kawasaki shares pearls of wisdom from the front lines of Silicon Valley about how to pitch, raise capital, and launch companies.

Takeaways

- The pitch deck is the central component of a business plan. Create your pitch deck first and use it to develop other materials.
- You will also need a financial model, and you'll include charts from that model in your presentation.
- In most cases you won't need a term-paper-style, text-based business plan, so don't waste your time writing one.

Learn more at upstartbootcamp.com

CHAPTER 3

Degrees of Planning

Different types of startups have different business planning needs.

Some startups don't need to create a presentation at all. This includes companies that won't grow beyond one person and won't ever raise capital. If you fall into this group, I recommend going through the research and analysis—the thinking behind a plan—but keeping your output very basic. For example, a few bullet points about each of the topics in a plan should suffice. Forget about the fancy graphics and charts.

If you have more than one founder, want to get feedback on your plan, or intend to raise capital, you'll need a presentation. Still, demands will vary.

Many startups raise capital from friends and family. These investors tend to be fairly easygoing. Chances are good that your wealthy Uncle is investing in your business because he loves you, wants to help you succeed, and thinks you are the greatest nephew this side of the Mississippi. He's not going to grill you. Still, the more you explain to him, the more informed he'll be—which means he'll be able to do more to help you (e.g. make appropriate introductions)—and the better he'll understand the challenges and risks you'll face using his money.

Other startups raise capital from angel investors—people who invest their own money on an amateur basis. Angels that invest in many startups or that are part of angel groups or "networks" tend to see many business plans and have high standards. If you are pitching to angels, you'll need to have a great presentation.

Finally, some startups raise money from VCs. If you are pitching to VCs, you'll need a comprehensive, investor-grade business plan backed up with detailed research and analysis.

Takeaways

- Simple startups should go through the thinking behind a business plan, but don't need to create fancy presentations.
- If you are raising capital, you'll need to craft a persuasive presentation—a sales document with tight logic and enough detail to back up your arguments. The more sophisticated your audience, the more comprehensive and professional your presentation should be.

Learn more at upstartbootcamp.com

CHAPTER 4

Spend Just Enough Time On Your Plan, And Not A Moment More

Regardless of why you are writing your business plan, it's important to strike a balance between planning and acting.

In most cases you should be able to develop a business plan pitch in about three weeks—about half the time you'd spend writing 40+ pages of prose. Here are a few problems that can arise from planning too much:

- **Wasted time.** Your business plan will change as you get advice and feedback and get your business up and running. If you get bogged down in "analysis paralysis," you may lose momentum and use up time that would be better spent on launching. Worse yet, you might miss a window of opportunity, like being first to market in your space or locking up key relationships that block competitors.

- **Hampered flexibility.** If you get so obsessed with your plan that you fall in love with it, you may be reluctant to modify your approach.

In fact, when your plan is about 80-percent finished, STOP! Don't obsess over making it perfect. Pitch it to a few people, just for feedback. The process of developing a business plan is iterative, after all. You can't develop a great plan in the basement of a library. You must make informed hypotheses and get out into the world to test them, by getting advice and by trying them out on real customers.

Look for patterns in the feedback, including parts of the deck that seem to confuse your audience, common questions, and concerns you hear multiple times. You are probably very close to the material, so try to step back and see your plan from another view. Analyze the feedback and tweak your plan accordingly. Try your best not to be defensive at this point. Instead, consider this to be good practice, and be grateful for the chance to make improvements.

 # Ask the Expert

Dany Levy: "A business plan should evolve."

Dany Levy is the founder and Editorial Director of DailyCandy, a daily newsletter with insider advice about style, food, fashion, and fun. Dany started DailyCandy in 2000 with a simple vision: one thing in your inbox telling you what to do that day. In 2008, Comcast acquired DailyCandy for a reported $125 million. Today DailyCandy has over three million subscriptions. Prior to founding DailyCandy, Dany worked for New York Magazine and Lucky, and wrote for The New York Times, Martha Stewart, and Vanity Fair. Dany is a graduate of Brown University.

UpStart: "How did you make use of a business plan at DailyCandy?"

Dany Levy: "A business plan should evolve depending on the stage of a business and on the audience it's written for. I started DailyCandy myself, at my kitchen table, with no employees. At that point, my business plan was just for me. It was a two page document describing what DailyCandy was, to help me clarify and narrow down what the product should be. That plan helped me stay focused, but it also left room for flexibility. I just concentrated on writing great editorial, and spreading the word. A year later, I developed a more comprehensive business plan, as I began to sell advertising and court suitors. Still, I kept it short. I figured investors needed to "get it" after the first few minutes. As the business grew, and I took on institutional investors, I needed more detail, like financial projections and strategies for marketing and sales."

UpStart: "Did developing a business plan provide any other benefits for you?"

Dany Levy: "Yes. Most of all, it helped me learn. That was one of the greatest things about building a business - the steep learning curve. And the business plan made that learning explicit. I got a lot of help with my plan from my CEO, Pete Sheinbaum. At the time, I handled editorial, and he handled business matters. I remember learning to measure the cost of acquiring customers, and the value of those customers. I think at the time one customer was worth somewhere around $10.37. The next time I attended a DailyCandy event, I looked around the room and imagined a price tag on every girl's head reading '$10.37'. Understanding the economics of the DailyCandy business gave me a much broader and deeper sense for what we were doing, and that ultimately paid off far beyond my wildest expectations."

Takeaways

- Plan too much, and you can waste valuable time. Don't plan enough, and you may overlook critical issues. Strike just the right balance between planning and action.

Learn more at upstartbootcamp.com

CHAPTER 5

This Is No Time To Delegate

The most important part of a business plan is the thinking behind it. A plan gives structure to that thinking and provides a way to present it, but going through the process of creating a plan is crucial.

I recently had a client named Penelope. As a seasoned executive in publishing, Penelope saw the foundation of the industry crumbling. She had a vision for a new type of publishing business and left her job to launch her own venture. She had great contacts and plenty of startup capital, but as an executive, Penelope had made the big-picture decisions, and had delegated execution to her capable minions. She wanted to create her business plan in the same manner—by paying me a lot of money to create a persuasive pitch. After a brief chat with Penelope, I could tell she hadn't thought through some key elements of her venture. So, much to her chagrin, we blocked out lots of time on her calendar to hit the white boards together. Eventually, Penelope came to realize the benefit of going through the analysis herself. By the time we finished her business plan presentation she knew it backward and forward, and when it came time to give the pitch to investors, it showed.

The lesson here is, by all means get help with your plan, but never hand it off to someone else. Here's why:

- You will be the one pitching the business plan, so you have to know it cold, including the reasoning behind each of your arguments. You will be pitching to people who know your industry very well; they are likely to ask you some very tough questions and challenge many of your points.

- You are the person developing the strategy for the business; you can't outsource your strategy. And your business plan must reflect your own personal vision. It has to reflect *your* entrepreneurial DNA.

- A business plan must be revised over and over. After nearly each pitch, you'll identify ways to improve it. Since you'll be the one updating the plan, you should know how it was developed in the first place.

Takeaways

- Get help with your business plan if necessary, but don't outsource the work altogether. You must go through the planning process yourself.
- The thinking behind the plan is more important than the plan itself.

Learn more at upstartbootcamp.com

CHAPTER 6

Wear Two Hats

Planning a venture and making a slide presentation about that venture are, of course, very different tasks. However, the topics or points covered are the same. Later in the book, I'll explain each of these topics, but first, let's look at how you'll use them. I like to think of it as wearing two different hats:

Hat 1: Investor Hat. With this hat on, you'll be assessing your potential business the way an investor would. After all, you'll be investing your time, money, and reputation on the venture, so you need to be sure it's viable. You must be objective while wearing this hat, to make certain you aren't about to take undo risk. Let's say you are working on the slide describing your team. Try to forget for a moment that you are talking about yourself and others about whom you have strong feelings. Ask yourself pointed questions like: "What are the profiles of the ideal people to play each role?" and "When do I need each of these people?" Not sure of the answers? This is the time to conduct research and analysis and get input from outside sources.

Food for Thought

Not all advice is created equal. Before you seek advice from someone, be sure to think about what that person knows and doesn't know.

You may want to get advice from people with expertise in particular job functions (e.g. sales, manufacturing, or technology), or with deep industry experience. If you haven't started a business before, you may also want advice from someone who has.

Try to find people with expertise that's relevant to your specific challenges. If you need to learn about selling expensive products to large corporations, someone with retail sales expertise may steer you in the wrong direction.

Beware of taking advice from people who can't see beyond outdated industry models—for example, someone in publishing who doesn't see how e-books, blogs, and Apple may change the rules of the publishing game.

As you answer these questions objectively, you'll get a better sense of whether your existing team is capable of executing your idea. You might decide right then and there that the venture is not a good fit for your team. Or you might identify some holes you'll need to fill in your team. How will you fill those roles? Maybe you'll add someone to your advisory board, hire a freelancer for a temporary project, or start wooing a key employee you'll want to hire in six months when cash flow starts to kick in. Now you are thinking like an investor.

Hat 2: Sales Hat. If, and only if, you came up with a viable plan with your investor hat on, switch roles. Put on your sales hat and think about the best way to show your audience what you figured out on your own. Package your findings in a way that forms a convincing argument, and use the data from your research and analysis to support that argument. Now that you can see the flaws and challenges, point them out in a proactive way, followed by the solutions you've developed.

 Word of Caution

Beware of "drinking the Kool-Aid"—getting so excited about your idea that you lose the ability to be impartial. Be sure to research and analyze your venture objectively before you get caught up in the fervor and start to pitch it.

The process for developing the slides is simple[5]:

1. Put 15 or so sheets of blank paper on a table. You'll transition to your computer later, but early on, paper helps with speed (no formatting to worry about) and flexibility—the cornerstones of this book's business planning philosophy.

2. Write one of the key points on the top of each piece of paper (e.g. Team). Underneath it, list the key questions you'll need to answer (I'll run you through the questions in the chapters to come).

3. Some questions will be easy to answer. Others will require more work; these questions will serve as your to-do list for research and analysis.

4. As you crunch through each of the slides, don't worry about your writing quality or formatting—just bullet out your logic and doodle a chart where appropriate.

5. When you've answered most of the questions, begin to create your slides on the computer.

---

5   Visit upstartbootcamp.com for advice, coaching and classes on developing business plans.

Takeaways

- Planning a venture and developing a slide presentation are very different tasks, but cover many of the same topics.
- As you consider each topic (e.g. marketing, team, financials), start by looking at your venture the way an investor would— with scrutiny and objectivity.
- Next, think like a salesperson and present your arguments in a persuasive manner.

Learn more at upstartbootcamp.com

CHAPTER 7

Business Plan Style

Before we get into the content of your pitch deck, here are some tips on style:

Be persuasive. Your slide deck is a sales document. Design it to persuade, not to inform. If there's a slide that just informs, give it a spin so it helps you *sell*. Remember that your pitch is a story. You have to hook the audience on the first slide and keep them interested all the way to the end. You have only one chance to do that with each pitch recipient.

Cater to your audience. Keep in mind the level of knowledge your audience has and what they really want to know. Make sure every point you make will be of interest to them. The book *Presenting to Win* makes an excellent case for looking at each slide from your audience's perspective and asking yourself, "So what?" That's a great reality check.

Keep it simple. Most of the message should come directly from your mouth, not from the slides. On your slides, use only the words you really need and keep the visuals simple. You are creating a pitch that you will present in person (or by phone), not a standalone document. You can create a leave-behind version with bullets that back up the points on your deck, but don't hand it out until you are finished presenting. Cut out the consultant-speak and acronyms and use simple, plain language. A good rule of thumb is to make sure even your mom would understand your pitch. Lose the busy charts—your visuals should make it easier to convey your points, not harder. Get rid of the corporate logo and contact info on every slide—once is enough. And see the recommended reading list at the end of this chapter for more advice.

 Food for Thought

5 Business Plan No-Nos....

1. Don't jump on the latest fad. I've seen entrepreneurs try to explain that they don't have to worry about competition because they will create a "Blue Ocean" or "Purple Cow." Eye-rolls nearly always ensue.

2. Don't be afraid of white space. A slide with one photo can be far more persuasive than a slide with seven bullet points. Resist the urge to cram every supporting fact into your deck. Prioritize and keep it simple and clean.

3. Don't try to show how much business lingo you know or explain ideas in complex ways. If your mom wouldn't understand what you are saying, simplify it until she would.

4. Don't forget you are planning a business, not just a product. If you spend 20 minutes on your entire presentation, don't spend more than three or four minutes on the product or service offering.

5. Don't send your plan out ahead of time or expect it to make sense without you there to explain it. A presentation is for presenting. A one-pager is for reading. A hybrid is for the garbage can.

Make it brief. Your pitch deck should consist of about 15 slides. It should take you about 20 minutes to deliver. That will leave plenty of time for discussion and will avoid boring or overloading your audience. Add as many backup slides as you want. You can always drill down on topics the audience wants to know more about.

More resources:

Presentation Zen: Simple Ideas on Presentation Design and Delivery by Garr Reynolds. You'll never look at a presentation the same way after reading this book. Reynolds walks you through the process of developing a pitch (e.g. never start on the computer) and helps you craft a presentation that has immediate and lasting impact. He also shoots down a lot of ill-conceived conventions (e.g. forget the background graphics, logos, and other useless clutter-contributors; white space is your friend).

Presenting to Win: The Art of Telling Your Story by Jerry Weissman. Weissman is a master at crafting persuasive presentations with back-to-back arguments that make audiences think "aha!" His tips are simple but essential (e.g. consider every point you make from an audience's perspective and ask yourself "why should they care?").

Takeaways

- Your deck is a sales document. Make sure it has a persuasive tone.
- Consider the interests and knowledge of your audience when preparing each slide. Ask yourself why they should care, or "So what?"
- Keep your deck short—ideally no more than 15 slides. Use simple, clear language and visuals. Add detail with your spoken words and backup slides.

Learn more at upstartbootcamp.com

CHAPTER 8

Warm-Ups

When I first started running workshops, I tried a two-step process that didn't work. First, I'd spend one session teaching founders how to develop each of the 15 elements of their business plan. Then I'd give them about two weeks to create a rough draft. After that, we'd get together so I could review the drafts. Unfortunately, most of the drafts were mediocre. For people new to the process, the task of going from nothing to a full presentation was a bit too difficult. In time, I realized the importance of taking a few interim steps.

The most effective of these steps are mini-business-planning exercises. I've included two of these exercises below. By completing them, you'll establish the foundation of your business plan. When we move on to drafting each of the 15 elements later in the book, you'll have a distinct advantage.

Exercise 1: WordPlay.
This exercise was inspired by a game I played as a kid— MadLibs— where you have to fill in the blanks in a story. It helps boil down your business idea to a simple statement. Simplicity will help clarify your vision and keep you laser-focused. It also will help you communicate your vision effectively and get others to agree with you. Try the exercise yourself:

- First, write down the customers you will target. Be specific. "Women ages 24-55" is too broad—you can do better than that. Consider the way your customers behave and the way they would define themselves. For example, the target for UpStart Bootcamp is "Entrepreneurs learning to write business plans, build teams, raise capital, and/or launch new companies." Write your answer here:_____

  _____

  _____

- Now, write the name of your product or brand. If you haven't figured that out yet, use a working title that you'll replace later. Mine is "UpStart Bootcamp". Go ahead: _____

  _____

  _____

- Next, define your product or service in the clearest way possible. It doesn't have to be sexy. You can doctor it up later for the purpose of pitching. First you need to get it right. The definition for UpStart Bootcamp is "an online school for startups." Write yours here: _____

  _____

  _____

- Next, explain how your product or service is unique. To do this well, put yourself in the shoes of your customers. How would *they* say you are different from other companies *they'd* consider to be your competitors? For UpStart Bootcamp, I'd say: "emphasizes speed, flexibility, and capital efficiency, delivered in a way that's inexpensive, easy, and inspirational." Your turn again: _____

  _____

  _____

- Next, put the pieces together, and you'll have a positioning statement you can use on the "Strategy" slide in your business plan pitch deck. For UpStart Bootcamp, it would read: "For entrepreneurs learning to write business plans, build teams, raise capital, and/or launch new companies, UpStart Bootcamp is an online school about startups that emphasizes speed, flexibility, and capital efficiency, delivered in a way that's inexpensive, entertaining and convenient." Your turn:_____

_____

_____

- Finally, simplify the message even more, to create your elevator pitch. Here's how it sounds for UpStart Bootcamp: "UpStart Bootcamp is an online school that teaches entrepreneurs how to plan and launch companies with speed and flexibility." Your turn:_____

_____

_____

Exercise 2: Situation / Complication / Resolution.

This exercise helps build the logic flow that will explain what you are planning to do and why it's a good idea—the cornerstone of your business plan.

- The first part is the situation—or why you feel there's an attractive opportunity. Ideally, you want a market that's big enough to sustain your goals, and trends that are in your favor. For UpStart Bootcamp, I'd write: "Best practices for planning, launching and growing startups have changed over the past ten years. Today's founders rent tech instead of creating it, bootstrap through early stages before raising capital, take advantage of web-based marketing, and plan with speed and flexibility." Write yours below:

_____

_____

_____

_____

_____

_____

- The second part is the complication—or why your customers are not getting what they need today. For UpStart Bootcamp, I'd write: "Venture capital seeking tech startups in places like Silicon Valley know the best practices. But there are over one million startups on Main Street that will never raise VC. They need ways to learn that are more helpful than books, and less expensive than MBA programs.." Okay, your turn:

  _____

  _____

  _____

  _____

  _____

- The last part is the resolution. It shows how you plan to satisfy the unmet needs of your customers from part two, and tap into the attractive opportunity from part one. If you did the WordPlay exercise earlier, you already have your answer. For UpStart Bootcamp, I'd write: "UpStart Bootcamp is an online school that teaches aspiring entrepreneurs to plan a new business with an emphasis on speed and flexibility. UpStart Bootcamp's classes are affordable, easy, and inspirational." Give it a shot:

  _____

  _____

  _____

  _____

  _____

More resources:

You can take an online class that covers these exercises and others at upstartbootcamp.com/classes. The classes are self-directed, so you can take them anytime, and most cost less than $100.

After completing the class, you can get feedback from an expert coach at upstartbootcamp.com/coaching. That way, you can make sure you are on the right track before moving on to develop your 15 slide business plan presentation.

Takeaways

- Most founders do a better job of drafting their business plan after completing mini-business-planning exercises.
- By running through these exercises, you'll establish a strong foundation of logic, upon which you can build a more impactful business plan.

Learn more at upstartbootcamp.com

CHAPTER 9

Pitch Deck Outline

Your business plan presentation should cover 15 topics. Here's an outline that should work for most business plan presentations:

SECTION	KEY POINTS
WHY YOU ARE DOING IT	1. **Goals**. What you hope to achieve and when you plan to achieve it.
WHAT YOU'LL DO	2. **Environment**. The market is big enough and is growing fast enough to sustain your goals, and the timing is right.
	3. **Customers**. Who you'll be selling to, specifically.
	4. **Unmet needs**. What your customers want that they can't get currently.
	5. **Strategy**. How you'll satisfy customer needs and establish your positioning within the market.
	6. **Analogs**. What you've learned from companies that have gone before you—both good and bad.

SECTION	KEY POINTS
HOW YOU'LL DO IT	7. **Offering**. Overview of your products or services.
	8. **Marketing**. How you will attract customers.
	9. **Business model**. How you will make money.
	10. **Team**. You have the right people for the job.
	11. **Risk**. What may go wrong and what you can do about it. What are your most serious competitive threats?
	12. **Progress**. What you've accomplished to-date.
	13. **Implementation plan**. What you'll do next, in phases.
	14. **Projections**. How, when, and to what extent cash will flow out and in.
WHAT YOU NEED	15. **Financing** (if you are raising capital). How much you need, when, for what, where it will get you, and how investors will benefit (e.g. your exit strategy). If you are not raising capital, use this section to spell out what you need (e.g. advice on XYZ, introductions to ABC, etc.

While there's some flexibility to this format, it's a good starting point for your analysis and your pitch. In the chapters that follow, I'll go through each point, explain how to conduct the necessary research and analysis, and explain how to present it—both on the slides and in-person.

Takeaways

- There's a set of topics every business plan should cover.
- In the chapters that follow, we'll delve into each topic in more depth.

Learn more at upstartbootcamp.com

Part Two:
The Pitch, Slide By Slide

This section of the book covers each slide in a business plan presentation. Typically, each slide covers a different one of the 15 topics in the outline.

In the chapters that follow, you'll learn to approach each topics in two ways. First, you'll act as an investor, assessing your business objectively. Then, you'll put on your sales hat, and craft a persuasive argument.

I'll use an example to illustrate the way one company might address each topic: DigitHeads. This company is fictitious, so don't get hung up on the facts used to present it—they are made up. Don't worry about whether the company has a viable idea, or if they operate in an industry that's different from yours. Instead, look at the way DigitHeads' founders think about and present their ideas, as a way to inform your own approach.

DigitHeads is a startup conceived by two founders, Lee Richards and Amanda Stevens. Their strategy is to provide inexpensive, remote tech support to people over the age of 45. Lee and Amanda worked together previously and decided to leave their jobs to start their own business. Their immediate plan is to raise $400,000 from angel investors so they can get the business to the point where it is generating significant revenue.

Goals

A business plan helps you—and people you seek advice or capital from—understand and assess your startup. But in order to conduct that evaluation and determine the best path to success, everyone involved must understand and agree upon what constitutes success. The best place to define this is up-front.

You won't find a "goals" slide in most pitches to venture capital firms. That's because founders and VCs already know the goal—to create a company that can be sold or taken public within five years for a massive amount of money—typically $100,000,000 or more. Why? Venture capital firms invest their funds in portfolios of companies. Some of those companies will flat-out fail. Others may become moderately successful. So each portfolio company must have the possibility of being so successful that it makes up for the rest of the investments. Entrepreneurs raising VC backing also need their venture to hit it *big*. Because founders give up a lot of ownership when they take VC investments, the entire pie has to turn out to be very large in order for their small slice to provide a big payoff.

Only a few startups raise millions in venture capital funding; actually, more people become new lottery millionaires each year in the U.S.![6] Many more get funding from angels. The vast majority of startups are bootstrapped—launched with less than $100,000, often provided by the founders themselves, along with their friends and family members.

Companies Launched Per Year and How They Are Funded[7][8][9]

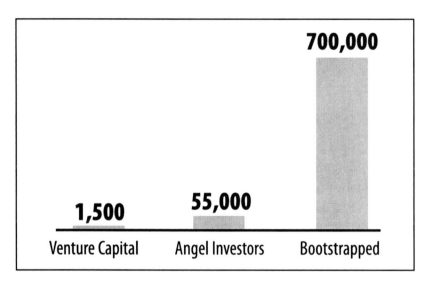

1,500	55,000	700,000
Venture Capital	Angel Investors	Bootstrapped

If you are bootstrapping or raising angel capital, you should make your goals explicit and make sure everyone involved knows the intended end-game and timing. Here's why:

---

6   TLC television show, "The Lottery Changed My Life"

7   PriceWaterHouseCoopers/National Venture Capital Association MoneyTree report, 2009. In 2008, venture capital firms in the U.S. invested in just 483 startup / seed stage companies, and 1,072 early-stage companies.

8   The Angel Investor Market in 2008, The Center for Venture Research, University of New Hampshire

9   US Census Bureau, Business Dynamics Statistics

- **Founder alignment**. If you have more than one founder, you need to make sure everyone agrees on what constitutes a "win." For example, I've seen situations where a pair of founders got a buyout offer for their company sooner than expected. One founder wanted to sell right there and then and the other wanted to grow the company for a few more years with the hope of selling for much more money. I've also seen startups where one founder defined success in terms of credibility and recognition, and another defined it in terms of financial returns. Chaos ensued in both cases.

- **Exit strategy**. Founders and investors must define and agree upon how and when they plan to turn their equity into cash or liquid stock, and how much they'll need to be satisfied. A sophisticated angel investor may be looking to turn a $50,000 investment into $1 million in cash within five years, while your wealthy uncle may be happy just to help you out and get a modest return at some unspecified point in the future.

- **Assessment**. Anyone giving you advice or feedback needs to understand what you are trying to accomplish. The same strategy may look great if your goal is to generate $1 million per year in revenue, and awful if your goal is to generate $50 million.

There are many different types of goals for startups; here are two of the most common:

1. **Harvesting profits**. A lot of people start companies in order to make a living doing something they enjoy over the long haul. A small public relations firm might follow this model. The PR firm's founders are looking to build a business that pays them well and provides them with jobs. They don't need to show rapid growth in order to make themselves attractive to companies that might want to acquire them, so they don't need to plow profits back into marketing or product development. They may never get acquired—but they don't really care. They live off the

business as an ongoing concern. They probably won't need to raise much capital, either.

2. **Building to scale and flip.** Other people are willing to sacrifice in the short-term for the possibility of a big payoff down the road. Founders of firms like this don't pay themselves much over the years, but they could make big money if the company is acquired. These entrepreneurs need to understand what type of companies the big guys like to acquire, the performance level they demand, and how much they pay for the companies they buy.

 Reality Check

What are your top three reasons for starting this venture?

1._____

2._____

3._____

If you have partners (and you probably should), what are their top three reasons for being involved?

1._____

2._____

3._____

Are you counting on this business to pay for your lifestyle and / or to support your family over the next few years? How much will that cost? Is it reasonable to assume you can pull enough out of the company to pay these costs?

_____

_____

Are you looking for a big financial windfall from selling your company or taking it public down the road? If so, what is your exit strategy?

If you are raising capital, how will you provide investors with a return on their investment—including targets for when and how much?

Lee and Amanda, founders of our fictitious example DigitHeads, create this slide for the Goals topic:

digitheads

- Founders: Lee Richards and Amanda Stevens
- DigitHeads provides tech support for people over 45
- Seeking $500,000 seed capital
- 5 year goal: $10 million revenue, sell for $75 million+

Here's what they say when presenting their Goals slide:

- "I'm Lee Richards and this is Amanda Stevens. We're the founders of DigitHeads, which is a consumer service that helps people over the age of 45 with technology challenges."

- "We've developed a working prototype, using capital from our savings and from friends and family investors."

- "Our next step is to raise $500,000. That will get us through 12 months of operations and let us hit some specific revenue goals we'll cover later."

- "Our end-game is to build a business we can sell for more than $75M within five years."

Takeaways

- Setting goals helps ensure that all your hard work has the potential to pay off in the way you, your teammates, and (if you are raising money) your investors want.
- Making your goals explicit provides a lens through which your advisors can give you feedback.

Learn more at upstartbootcamp.com

Environment

This part of the plan is about ensuring that you'll be operating in a favorable environment.

Here are a few issues to consider. Remember to start out wearing your investor hat so you can make an objective evaluation before you try to convince others you are right:

- **Size.** How big is the market, in aggregate? Is it big enough to support your goals for the company? One way to think about this is to consider your revenue goals five years out. Are you trying to build a $10 million revenue business? A $100 million revenue business? What is your best estimate of how big the total market will be in five years, measured by revenues? Dividing the total market size by your revenues gives you market share. Does the share you'll need to hit your goals seem reasonable, in light of the time and money it took for competitors to hit similar milestones?

- **Segments.** To figure out just how big your pie is, you'll need to define the groups or "segments" of customers you will target. Together, these groups represent your "total *addressable* market." To find the total addressable market for your business, think of the most meaningful ways to break the market down into segments. Look at factors such as demographics, geography, price, distribution channels, or buying habits.

 Word of Caution

Sometimes entrepreneurs size up their opportunity by saying, "This is a $1.5 billion market. It's huge! If we capture just one percent, we'll have a $15 million business." The problem is, the $1.5 billion market size is pretty much irrelevant because it includes lots of segments that have nothing to do with your business. The part of the market you care about is the part you can sell to—the *addressable market*. That's the amount of revenue your company could generate if you got 100 percent of your potential customers.

For example, let's say you are starting a cosmetics business, selling high end products ("prestige" in industry parlance) through U.S. specialty stores like Saks, Sephora and Neiman Marcus. Total annual a sales of cosmetics may be more than $40 billion on a global basis, but that's not your opportunity. You won't be selling lipsticks at Wal Mart, for example. Instead, you'll compete in the U.S. market for "prestige" cosmetics, which is closer to $3 billion in revenue.

It may seem like bigger is better, but overstating the market opportunity is bad for everyone. It can mislead founders and shareholders, who will be disappointed when sales are lower than expected. It can also reflect poorly on founders, especially when pitching to investors who know better.

Reality Check

What specific groups of customers will you target (your addressable market)?

_____

_____

How much is your addressable market spending today, measured by revenue?

_____

_____

How fast is your total addressable market growing?

_____

_____

What are the top three trends driving growth in your industry?

1._____

2._____

3._____

- **Growth.** A big market is great. A big, *growing* market is even better. When a market is growing, there are more customers all the time and less competition for each customer. Many venture capital firms look for opportunities to invest within big markets that are in the early stages of rapid growth.

- **Trends.** When industries are stable, big entrenched companies tend to have the advantage. But sometimes the balance of power gets shaken up, giving fast-moving, flexible startups a fighting chance. Technology developments, economic swings, consumer trends, and government policies are among the forces that drive such industry shake-ups. What's going on in your target industry and how will that impact your chances of success? In other words, why does it make sense to launch your business *now*? To learn more about market dynamics, read *Competitive Strategy* by Michael Porter, cited at the end of this chapter.

Many sources of data are available that can be helpful for estimating market size, growth and trends. Market research companies like Gartner Group, Forrester Research, and NPD Group publish reports about certain industries, with great statistics. Unfortunately, these reports tend to cost thousands of dollars, so you may have to get creative. Here's one trick: research companies often publish highlights of their studies in their free press releases, which you can access from their online press release archives. Industry associations, industry experts, suppliers, and competitors are other good sources of information.

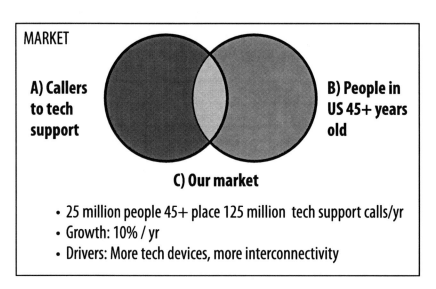

Lee's comments when showing this slide:

- "Our primary market is people in the United States over the age of 45 who call tech support for live help with technology challenges. That includes 25 M Americans, placing 125 M tech support calls per year."

- "The market is growing at over 10% per year."
- "Growth is driven by two things: the population is aging and technology in our daily lives is proliferating. We have more devices, more applications, and they are all expected to work together."

More resources:

Competitive Strategy: Techniques for Analyzing Industries and Competitors by Michael E. Porter. When it comes to understanding strategy, this book is the bible. Porter lays out classic frameworks, like the "five forces analysis," that help you evaluate the attractiveness of industries, considering barriers to entry, the relative power of buyers and suppliers, the availability of substitutes, and the intensity of rivalry. It's required reading at most top MBA programs.

Takeaways

- If possible, demonstrate that you will compete in a market that is large enough to sustain your goals and that the market is growing.
- When you consider market size, be sure to limit the universe to segments that are truly relevant to your business—your total addressable market.
- Explain what currently drives growth in your market. Ideally you should be taking advantage of these growth drivers.

Learn more at upstartbootcamp.com

Customers

Who are your potential customers, and what do they need? Answering these questions will help you build a better product or service offering, and attract customers more efficiently.

Putting your customers into groups or segments with similar characteristics is also helpful. That way, you can decide which segments to go after first, create different offerings or pricing policies to meet their needs, and reach each segment most cost-effectively. Here are a few ways to segment your customers:

Demographics. Sometimes it's helpful to segment a market based on demographic variables like age, sex, income, geographic location, nationality, education level, race, religion, or occupation. The AARP targets people by age group, for example, while Fidelity probably cares more about income or wealth.

Psychographics. These are factors like values, interests or lifestyle. Polo Ralph Lauren sells clothing and accessories, but they also sell a dream of old-money elegance and luxury. The Body Shop sells beauty and skin care products, but they also sell the benefits of a healthy conscience, because they support fair trade, donate to charity, and do not test on animals.

Behaviors. Some companies segment customers based on behavior, like how often they buy / use a product, the extent to which they tend to be loyal to particular brands, or the specific benefits they are looking for. Nike makes and markets certain shoes for hard-core athletes and different shoes for people who just want stylish footwear. AT&T has different calling plans for people who spend more time on the phone or make more calls from international locations.

Once you've identified your target segments, take a closer look at each one, including:

- **Size.** How many people are in this group? To what extent is the group growing or shrinking?

- **Needs.** Are there specific things that nearly all members of a specific segment need?

- **Influencers.** Do the members of your market segments take cues from other people or groups? Does a teenager wear what her favorite actress wears? Does a mom buy the cereal her son asks for?

- **Trends.** How are more general trends impacting your specific target segments? Twitter may be huge with 40-something techies, but of little interest among college kids.

- **Decision-making.** Who makes the buying decisions? Are they made by one person? Is it a multi-step process? How long does it typically take? What factors are most important? Are there people in an organization who might feel threatened by a new product or service? Is there someone within an organization you could win over to help shepherd you through the sales process?

- **Loyalty.** Once members of a target segment make a purchase, how likely are they to buy the same brand in the future?

Reality Check

What are the most important defining characteristics of your customers—things about them that make them a perfect fit for the product or service you'll offer?

_____

_____

What different groups of customers will you serve?

1._____

2._____

3._____

What are the particular needs of each of these customer groups? How do they differ from one another?

1._____

2._____

3._____

How are each of these customer groups satisfying their needs today?

1._____

2._____

3._____

Here's how Lee and Amanda from DigitHeads assess and pitch their primary market segments:

CUSTOMERS

- Our customers are "digital immigrants" – people 45+ learning to use technology
- Growth: 10% per year
- Digital immigrants need hand-holding

Lee's talking points for this slide are as follows:

- "Our customers are over 45 and have frustrations with basic tech challenges. They're called "Digital Immigrants" because they didn't learn technology in school, or for fun—they had to learn to keep up with kids and colleagues. Now they're surrounded by it, from computers, smart phones, and digital cameras, to iPods, DVRs, and Web sites."

- "They grew up reading the instructions and calling for help. But today's tech is more DIY-oriented and support is more automated. That frustrates them. Just consider how many times you've received a call from a parent or in-law asking for help with technology."

More resources:

Market Customization: Market Segmentation, Targeting, and Positioning, Harvard Business Press. You can buy this as a standalone chapter and download the PDF for less than $10. It's a good little overview of how to think about meaningful groups of customers and address them in effective ways.

Takeaways

- Identify your specific target customer segments and make sure they have important needs that are not being satisfied today.
- Back up your argument with quotes from credible sources, third-party market research, and/or your own market research.

Learn more at upstartbootcamp.com

Unmet Needs

Once you've identified your target customer segments, prove that members of those segments have needs that are not being fulfilled today. It's especially important to assess this component of your business idea objectively. I recently bought business cards online from Moo[10]. I particularly liked the design that featured this image on the back of the card:

If I had a dollar for every entrepreneur I've met who says "I just know this is a great idea," I'd be loaded. Just because *you* think there's an unmet need and your friends and family agree with you, doesn't make it true. Here are a few ways to prove with objectivity that there are unmet customer needs:

---

10 http://us.moo.com/en/

- Find credible authorities stating that there's a gap in the market. Those could include industry leaders, research analysts, or journalists.

- Obtain market research conducted by a reputable firm like NPD Group, IDC, Forrester Research, or Gartner Group.

- Do your own research. One way to do this is to conduct a survey with a company like Zoomerang. You can craft a survey, pick a relevant target audience, and pay Zoomerang to get you a minimum number of completed surveys from your target demographic. It can cost upwards of $1,500, but within a day or two you can obtain data that will help you make a strong case for what customers really want but are not getting.

Once you are convinced that there are critical unmet needs, create a slide to support your contention. Remember, you are looking for head nods from your audience. It's important for them to believe your target customers have a real need. Soon you will unveil your product or service and you can't have potential investors thinking, "Yeah, customers might find that nice to have, but not essential." That's a deal-breaker. It's also critical for your audience to believe the demand is not being satisfied today.

 Word of Caution

A lot of entrepreneurs blow this topic in their business plan—because they're so close to the material, they think the answers are clear to others. When they are rejected they think, "That investor just didn't get it." But it's the entrepreneur who didn't "get it"—and by "it" I mean a check. To avoid this, put yourself in the shoes of your audience and expect them to be skeptical. Get feedback from people similar to those you'll be pitching. Remember that the hurdles are always higher when you are asking for someone's money than when you are asking for their feedback.

Reality Check

What customer needs are not being met today?

1._____

2._____

3._____

What evidence do you have for each of these unmet needs, other than personal experience and feedback from friends and family?

1._____

2._____

3._____

How are these unmet needs impacting your customers in ways that are important to them, such as by affecting their health, happiness, or wealth?

1._____

2._____

3._____

If these needs were satisfied, how would your customers be better off?

1._____

2._____

3._____

Lee and Amanda from DigitHeads show the following slide to demonstrate that there are unmet needs:

UNMET NEEDS

"There are millions of us Boomers, and we have money. Now that we are getting older, we need more services than ever. One service business you could start is Technical Support for Boomers. We're having a lot of trouble with technology these days."

~Dave Barry

- **Digital immigrants have specialized tech support needs that are not being met today. They need live, convenient, empathetic help with even the most basic tech challenges.**
- **66% would pay to have the right tech support solution.**

Here are Andy's comments on the slide:

- "Digital Immigrants need help with even the most basic tech challenges, like how to use their DVR, or Skype with their grandkids. They want that help to be live so they can ask questions, remote so it's convenient, and provided by people who can communicate with them well."

- "We weren't the first to identify this need. Here's a quote from an article published five years ago. But we conducted 400 surveys; 66% of the respondents said their tech support needs are not being met and that they'd pay $20 per month to have the right solution."

Takeaways

- In this part of the business plan, identify your specific target customer segments and make sure they have important needs that are not being satisfied today.
- Back up your argument with quotes from credible sources, third-party market research, and/or your own market research.

Learn more at upstartbootcamp.com

Strategy

The objective for this slide is to provide a clear statement of your company's reason for being, or over-arching strategy. You'll also want to demonstrate how you will satisfy the unmet needs of your customers and take advantage of the attractive market opportunity.

 Word of Caution

Boiling your company's reason for existence down to a simple, clear statement is tougher than it sounds, so many entrepreneurs botch this slide. Some try to squeeze too much information into it and end up trying to be all things to all people. Others fill the description with meaningless business jargon. Still others fail to explain how their product or service is differentiated in the market, using assertions like "we'll be the market leader" without explaining how.

The best way to tackle this challenge is with the WordPlay exercise from Chapter 8. Start with the MadLibs-type exercise and then massage your language so it flows more smoothly. Here's a quick reminder:

For:_____

(your specific target segment)

_____ is the

(your product name or brand)

_____

(definition of your product or service)

That _____

(unique point of difference)

 ## Ask the Expert

Chip Hazard: "I am often struck by how much trouble... founders have articulating their strategies in a clear, concise, compelling way."

Chip Hazard has been in venture capital for over 15 years and has an impressive track record of success. He's currently a general partner at Flybridge Capital Partners, a leading early-stage venture capital firm. He sits on the board of eight information technology companies. Previously, Chip served as general partner at Greylock Partners and was a consultant at Bain and Company. Chip is a graduate of Stanford University and The Harvard Business School—where we met—and where he graduated at the top of his class as a Baker Scholar and a Ford Scholar. You can read Chip's blog at www.hazardlights.net.

UpStart: "What advice do you have for entrepreneurs pitching their strategy?"

Chip Hazard: "As an early-stage venture capital investor, I regularly meet with entrepreneurs that are just getting their businesses off the ground. During these meetings I am often struck by how much trouble the founders have articulating their strategies in a clear, concise, compelling way. I encourage entrepreneurs to focus on delivering a simple vision of what they are trying to do and why it is important, what markets are being targeted and how broad these markets are, and how the idea, customer value proposition and market translate into a compelling business opportunity. It is important to avoid in this introduction the deep technical details of how the product or service works, but rather focus on the connection between a large unmet need and your unique solution. The MadLibs exercise outlined in this chapter is a great tool to drive this exercise, resulting in a simple, short, clear message."

UpStart: "Please provide an example of a great strategy summary."

Chip Hazard: "I always felt Skype did this well. Using your format, from the beginning their message was something like: For people who want to connect with friends and family around the world, Skype is a person-to-person Internet telephone service that is free, simple and easy to use."

Reality Check

Who is your target customer?

_____

What is your brand name?

_____

How would you define the product or service you are offering?

_____

_____

_____

How would one of your customers explain how your product or service is different from others that are available?

_____

_____

_____

Combine your answers to the four questions above and tweak the wording to form a sentence:

_____

_____

_____

Finally, tweak your answer again. This time, make it simple enough to explain to your mom. Then read it out loud and write it below:

_____

_____

_____

_____

Here's the DigitHeads strategy slide:

STRATEGY

digitheads

DigitHeads provides tech support for people over 45.
They can call DigitHeads at any time, with any tech-related
question or issue, and get help from well-informed,
well-spoken tech experts.

Here's what Lee says while showing this slide:

- "DigitHeads provides tech support for people who didn't grow up with technology."

- "We're like a tech-support concierge service. We provide live, remote, 24/7 help with basic tech challenges across all products and services."

- "We also cater to the specialized needs of the over-45 set. With DigitHeads, they don't encounter long hold times, confusing automated phone systems, or service reps they can't understand."

- What companies can serve as "analogs" —models that you want to follow since they've found the keys to success, or avoid because of the reasons they failed?

- Who can help you understand the real story of what worked and what didn't work with those models—and why or why not? Can you network your way to their investors? Founders? Employees? Ex-employees? Competitors or suppliers?

- Venture capitalists that specialize in the market you are pursuing tend to be particularly knowledgeable about analogs. Even if you are not planning to raise venture capital funding in the near term, you often can benefit from getting their perspective and speaking to their contacts.

Reality Check

What companies are useful analogs for yours?

1._____

2._____

3._____

What can you learn from things they've done well?

1._____

2._____

3._____

What can you learn from things they've done poorly?

1._____

2._____

3._____

How would you explain your idea to someone using the format of "we're the (this) of (that)?

We're the: _____

of: _____

ANALOGS

ThirdAge
- Web portal dedicated to people over 45
- 1million unique visitors / month
- Specialized content, simple navigation

Consumer Cellular
- Mobile phones for people 50+
- Senior-friendly phones and simple plans
- Exclusive partnership with AARP

Here's how Lee and Amanda discuss analogs for DigitHeads:

- "Third Age has built one of the biggest online communities for people over 45. They provide content and features that older people want, without making them feel old."

- "Consumer Cellular also caters to older people. They've forged a strong partnership with AARP to generate leads and have phones and plans that are easy for boomers and seniors to buy and use."

Takeaways

- When possible, find analogs for your business—examples of companies that have tried similar things.
- Find out what aspects of those analogs made them successful, or unsuccessful, and learn from them.
- Describing your company as "the (this) of (that)"—applying a model used elsewhere to your situation—can help clarify your strategy and boost investor confidence.

Learn more at upstartbootcamp.com

Offering

In this part of the business plan, you will explain what you'll be selling to your customers. Here are a few things to consider:

- What's the best product or service to sell initially? Let's say you are starting a clothing company. Will you start with t-shirts? That might impact where you sell the products—for example, some retailers might require a mix of products from new suppliers. It also could have a lasting impact on how customers view your brand; they might continue to think of you as a t-shirt company long after you've developed a much more extensive product assortment.

- How will your offerings evolve over time? Will you expand by providing different categories of products, like jeans? Will you increase the depth of your line by making t-shirts in more styles and colors? Will you add products at different price points? License your brand to other companies to make accessories or fragrances?

- What's the rationale behind your product evolution? Are you keeping your offerings limited at first, in order to hit certain milestones before spending too much money? Establishing a platform that will make it possible to expand? This is a good time to refer back to the analogs. Chances are good that there are some best practices from which you can learn.

Once you've completed your analysis, think about a simple, clear way to explain it to your audience. If you are pitching to investors, this is the time to get them excited. You've appealed to their logic so far; now get their emotions involved. Wheel out visuals if you have them. If you are in the fashion business, show a video of your last fashion show, along with music that will ramp up the energy in the room. If you are building a food or beverage company, let them see, smell, and taste the product.

 Word of Caution

Many entrepreneurs overdo this element of their presentation, thinking that their product/service description should take up the lion's share of their pitch. Investors *do* want to make sure you have a great offering, but at this point, they want to learn more about your business than about your product. Give them just the highlights and let them learn more later.

Reality Check

What products or services will you sell within the next six to nine months?

1._____

2._____

3._____

How will you expand your product or service offering over the following one to two years?

1._____

2._____

3._____

What will you do first? 1) sell a broader selection of products or services to your initial group of customers 2) sell a deeper array of product or service versions to your initial group of customers, or 3) sell existing products or services to new groups of customers.

_____

_____

Why do you think the expansion strategy you've just explained makes the most sense? Is it consistent with the way other successful companies in your industry have expanded?

_____

_____

_____

Lee and Amanda from DigitHeads start with a brief overview of their offerings. Then they show a few screen shots of their product and explain that they'll follow up with passwords, so audience members can see the site for themselves later.

PRODUCT OFFERING

FEATURES	BENEFITS
Live remote support, any time	Convenient. No waiting for business hours.
Well trained tech generalists	Effective. 75% of issues resolved within 10 minutes without transfers.
Remote login	Easy. For problems related to PCs, support staff can see, fix themselves.
$9.95 per month + premium service fees	Affordable. Most problems resolved within flat fee. Additional cost for bigger challenges, like crashes, viruses, or speeding up clogged hard drives.

Lee and Amanda's comments:

- "We designed DigitHeads to be easy, affordable, convenient and effective."

- "We solve 75% of user problems within 10 minutes, under the $9.99 flat fee, with no waiting to be transferred."

- "After this meeting, I'll give you a code you can use to log in to our Web site. It's still being tested, but you can get live help with PDAs, DVRs, and PCs between 9:00 a.m. and 6:00 p.m."

Takeaways

- With your investor hat on, think through the evolution of your product or service offering. What should you start with? How should you expand? Why? When?
- When pitching your offering to your audience, start with a simple overview.
- If applicable, show them a visual, such as a video, demo, or prototype. Step away from the slides and get your audience excited about your offering. Just don't overdo it—your offering shouldn't overshadow the rest of your pitch.

Learn more at upstartbootcamp.com

Marketing

Marketing is about creating a fit between your product or service offering and the needs of your customer segments, and getting customers in those segments to appreciate and act on that fit by using or buying what you are providing. Here are some issues to consider for the marketing section of your plan:

- **Pricing.** What is your pricing strategy? Here are a few examples:

  - ~ **Penetration pricing:** Set prices lower than those of competitors as a way to increase market share.

  - ~ **Skim pricing:** Set initial prices higher than those of competitors to signal that your quality is better, then drop them later.

  - ~ **Freebie pricing:** Give away a key component of your product to lock customers into your standard and then sell them products that fit (this is sometimes called "give away the razors to sell the blades"[12]).

---

12 Next time you walk into a drugstore, notice the prices on razors and blades. Also notice that there always seems to be a new-fangled razor touted to give you a closer shave than ever before, because it has (choose one or more of the following: moisture strips, more blades, a

- **Distribution.** How will you reach customers? In person, by phone, or online? Can you take advantage of "channel partners"—intermediaries who have an existing relationship with your customers? Be sure to explain how you will activate this type of relationship. If you want another company's sales force to sell your product, what kind of incentive will get them to really push your offering? If you want another Web site to promote your product and collect a share of the revenue they help generate, how exactly will they get the word out? What terms will they agree to? Have they done something similar before? How well did it work? Here are a few types of distribution partnerships:

  ~ **Retailers.** These could be online or physical. Building an iPhone application? Sell it through the Apple App Store, where thousands of customers go to find applications. Selling organic food? Land an account at Whole Foods.

  ~ **Resellers** (aka VARS, or Value-Added Resellers). If you sell software, you might develop a relationship with Web site developers or systems administrators who can recommend your products to their clients.

  ~ **Manufacturers.** Some manufacturers sell their products with components from other companies baked-in, like GPS systems in cars, bleach in laundry detergent, or software on computers. Other manufacturers partner with companies that sell add-ons such as accessories made expressly for your brand of baby stroller.

  ~ **Affiliates.** Let's say you sell concert and sporting event tickets that appeal primarily to college students. You might want to negotiate affiliate deals with Websites that

---

motor inside, etc). The new razor will probably have a reasonable price tag. But soon after you're hooked on the new model, you'll need new blades for it (it came with only one), and that's where you'll start forking over the big bucks.

already have amassed legions of college students, having the Web site promote your tickets in exchange for a share of revenues.

- **Advertising and promotion.** How will you promote the product? Maybe you will buy keywords on Google, set up booths at trade shows, run a local public relations campaign tied to your product launch, or provide in-store tastings. Perhaps you'll establish yourself as a thought leader, speak at conferences, write a blog, cultivate a loyal base of e-mail subscribers, and update your followers via Twitter, Facebook, and LinkedIn. Don't just list potential tactics; do your homework to find out if the deals, terms, and expected results are realistic.

You could also focus this slide on a specific type of challenge you expect to face. For example, if building a large subscriber base is a key success factor, focus on how you'll do that. If you will sell through retailers, show which accounts you plan to land and how many stores you'll be in. If your plan is to offer a range of products and trade buyers up from inexpensive options to more expensive ones, lay out the process you envision. Or maybe your business hinges on a "pyramid of influence." One of my clients in the cosmetic business found that the key to building a consumer following was getting top makeup artists to believe in, use, and talk up her products. Those makeup artists influenced the taste-makers—people like beauty bloggers, beauty editors, models, and stylists who have their own consumer following.

Reality Check

What's your pricing strategy, and why?

_____

Will you sell to customers directly, or through intermediaries like retailers or wholesalers? If the latter, which ones are most critical?

_____

What do you expect to be the top three ways you will make customers aware of your product or service?

1._____

2._____

3._____

Will you make use of promotions such as discounts, free trials, gifts with purchase, or sampling?

_____

Will you advertise your products or services? If so, where and how?

_____

_____

Will you attempt to generate press? If so, what are your dream press opportunities (e.g. appearance on Oprah, front page of the New York Times business section)?

1._____

2._____

3._____

DigitHeads founders show this slide:

MARKETING

METHOD	TACTICS
Distribution Channels	Partnership with AARP with promotions on Web site and in monthly magazines
Publicity	PR campaign to focus on morning TV, major metro newspapers
Promotion	Free accounts for leaders of influential organizations
Advertising	Test Google keyword buys (e.g. "blackberry help")

Lee's comments:

- "We have a letter of intent from AARP. As long as we launch on time, they'll give us a six-month window as a test. They'll feature us on pages in their Web site, which has over 1M unique visitors per month, and in a magazine that reaches 5M subscribers each month."

- "We'll run our PR internally, as we have in the past with success. For DigitHeads, we'll focus on media consumed by our target customers, like newspapers and morning shows."

- "We'll also test keyword buys and free subscriptions for thought leaders."

More resources:

Inbound Marketing, by Brian Halligan and Darmesh Shah. In this book, the entrepreneurial authors argue that outbound marketing tactics are ineffective and outdated (e.g. e-mail blasts, direct mail, television commercials, print ads and trade shows) and that inbound marketing tactics have taken their place. For example, Web sites that get users to contribute to conversations and act as hubs for action that takes place on industry blogs, Google, and social media sites. The book provides results-oriented advice that helps entrepreneurs get more customers with less money.

The Tipping Point, by Malcolm Gladwell. This book seeks to explain how and why ideas and products spread and become "hits." Gladwell divides the world into "mavens" who figure out what's great, "connectors" who bring people together, and "salesmen" who spread the gospel. It's an interesting look at word-of-mouth marketing—the holy grail for cash-strapped startups.

Takeaways

- Use this section of the business plan to map out your marketing plan.
- One approach is to summarize your goals and approach in each major area of marketing, such as your pricing, distribution, product line development, target market, and promotion.
- Another approach is to focus on how you'll address a specific challenge that will be critical to successfully marketing your product or service.

Learn more at upstartbootcamp.com

Business Model

Business model is a fancy term for "how a company makes money." Later we'll address financial projections, which are about estimating how the numbers for your venture will play out on a big-picture basis. For the business model slide, you should focus on "unit" economics—predicting and measuring numbers pertaining to one customer and/or one transaction (e.g. a sale).

The type of calculations required to analyze a business model are simple. In fact, they are often called "back-of-the-envelope" calculations, since all you need is a piece of paper, a pen, and a basic calculator. But don't let the simplicity fool you; back-of-the-envelope calculations are as important for a startup as any sophisticated set of financial projections; they let you break down the complex challenge of predicting financial performance into bite-sized pieces. Also, if you are trying to raise money, looking at the back-of-the-envelope numbers correctly during this part of the presentation sets the right stage for your discussion of financial projections in the future. Before getting to the numbers, there are two things to consider.

First, determine how you will generate revenue. At some point during the development of commerce, companies simply made or bought products for one price and sold them for a higher price.

Business models have gotten more complicated over time, with innovation. Here are just a few examples:

BUSINESS MODEL	HOW IT WORKS	EXAMPLES
Subscription fees	Customers pay recurring, flat fees	Equinox fitness Netflix
Franchise	One company establishes a format, and franchisees pay to apply it locally with support	Subway Mail Boxes, Etc.
Listing fees	Consumers or companies pay to promote themselves or their products or services	Monster.com Personal ads
Marketplaces	A company collects a fee for connecting buyers and sellers	eBay Sotheby's
Media	A company provides content, attracts an auidence and then sells access to advertisers	NBC iVillage
Freemium	Basic offerings are provided for free, with the goal of selling premium products or services	LinkedIn "Ladies night"
Direct sellling	Companies recruit and train sales reps, who then sell to customers and earn commissions	Avon Amway

The second thing to consider before running your numbers is whether you:

1. Interact directly with your end customer (e.g. sell to customers via a sales force or your Web site, sell advertisers access to your customers), or

2. Work with intermediaries who interact with your end customer (e.g. retailers, distributors, resellers).

If your answer above is "1," you'll want to understand how much it will cost you to get one customer in the door and what that customer relationship is worth to your business. The relationship between those numbers—the cost of acquiring a customer and the lifetime value of a customer—can spell the difference between success and failure. If you are spending too much to attract new customers and not getting enough value from each one, you won't have a profitable business. Ideally, the value of a customer should be at least three times the cost of acquiring a customer. Here's how to do the math:

- What does it cost to acquire one customer? Look at the numbers for a set period of time, like six months of historical or projected operations.

  ~ A) What are the total costs of sales and marketing for those months, including marketing expenses, salaries and commissions of marketing staff?

  ~ B) How many new customers did you attract in those months?

  ~ C) What is A divided by B?

- What's the lifetime value of one customer?

  ~ D) How long is your relationship with an average customer?

  ~ E) How much revenue do you generate per customer, over your entire relationship with that customer?

  ~ F) What are the variable costs of delivering your products or services to an average customer, including the costs of service and support and the cost of employees providing the service and support?

  ~ G) E minus F is the lifetime value of a customer.

Digitheads answer is "1," so they present the following slide:

BUSINESS MODEL	
Estimated average cost to acquire one customer (direct costs of advertising plus salaries and benefits for marketing and PR staff)	$75.00
Estimated average revenue over the lifetime of a customer relationship (18 month subscription @ $9.95 +1 upsell service @ $125)	$304.00
Direct costs of delivering services / customer during the lifetime of the relationship	($78.00)
Lifetime value per customer	$226.00
Ratio of lifetime value to acquisition cost	3x

Here's what Lee from DigitHeads says while showing this slide:

- "We make money by selling monthly subscriptions for basic tech support for $9.95 and by selling premium services, like remote help setting up wireless networks and removing viruses, for $125."

- "This chart shows two numbers we plan to track closely. Right now they are just projections, but we based them on researching other similar companies."

- "We anticipate that it will cost $75 to acquire an average customer."

- "We think each customer will generate over $225 in margin— more than three times the acquisition cost."

What if your answer to the question about how you interact with customers is "2" —you work with intermediaries who interact with your end customers (e.g. retailers, distributors, resellers)? In that case, you probably won't know your cost of acquiring a customer or the lifetime value of a customer. If your business functions this way, there's another way to look at your business model. It's called "break-even volume," which determines how many units you'll need to sell in order to reach profitability. Here's the math:

- What's the unit contribution, or margin, generated by one sale or transaction?

  ~ A) What are the revenues from one transaction?

  ~ B) What are the costs linked directly to each transaction, aka "variable costs" (e.g. sales commissions and costs of producing the product, aka "cost of goods")?

  ~ C) What do you get by subtracting variable costs per transaction from revenue per transaction? The answer is your "unit contribution"—the amount each transaction contributes to covering your company's fixed costs, or overhead.

- What is your projected monthly overhead? Overhead consists of costs that don't vary directly with sales volume (e.g. rent, salaries, utilities, legal and accounting expenses, etc.). Typically it's helpful to project monthly overhead for a future period, such as after 12 months, rather than look at current overhead.

- How many units do you have to sell per month to cover your monthly overhead? Is that a realistic number?

Here's an example of how another fictitious company would address its business model. This company is called JuiceBox. JuiceBox sells organic fruit juice to retailers like Whole Foods, Publix and Safeway.

BUSINESS MODEL

Revenue from the sale of one bottle of juice	$1.50
Variable costs of selling each bottle (includes cost of goods, plus delivery and commissions)	$0.50
Unit contribution	$1.00
Average monthly overhead (after 1 year)	$20,000
Break-even volume	20,000

Here's how the founders of JuiceBox would pitch this slide:

- "We generate $1.50 in revenue for each bottle we sell to stores."

- "The cost of making and selling each bottle is $0.50."

- "After one year, we expect our monthly overhead to be $20,000."

- "We'll have to sell 20,000 bottles of juice per month to cover our overhead and break even. We expect to reach that volume 12 months after we raise capital."

 **Reality Check**

How will your company generate revenue?

_____

A year from now, what will your overhead expenses be per month?

_____

How much margin (revenue minus variable costs) does one transaction or sale generate?

_____

How many transactions will you need to cover your overhead on a monthly basis?

_____

If you sell directly to your customers, what will it cost you to acquire one customer —including the costs of marketing and sales staff?

_____

If you sell directly to your customers, how much margin do you expect one customer to generate for your business during the entire lifetime of your relationship with the customer (lifetime value per customer)?

_____

What's the lifetime value of one customer, divided by the cost of acquiring one customer? Hint: If the answer is below three, you may want to find ways to improve your business model.

_____

Ask the Expert

Bo Peabody: "Entrepreneurship is like a video game."

Bo Peabody is co-founder and Managing General Partner of Village Ventures, an early-stage venture capital firm. Previously, Bo founded / co-founded a string of startups, including: Tripod (one of the first social networks, later acquired by Lycos), Waterfront Media, VoodooVox, FullTurn Media, and UplayMe. He's also an owner of Mezze, Inc, which consists of three award-winning restaurants. Bo wrote a book for entrepreneurs called *Lucky or Smart?* published by Random House. He is a graduate of Williams College.

UpStart: "What advice do you have for entrepreneurs pitching investors about their business models?"

Bo Peabody: "Entrepreneurs have the counterintuitive task of having to think big and act small. For any business that is going to attract venture investors, a big vision is important. But that's the easy part. The much harder job is figuring out how to distill that vision into an actionable plan that has clear, incremental levels of success. Entrepreneurship is like a video game...you need to know what the levels are and then reach each one before going on to the next."

UpStart: "Are there particular business models that you prefer to invest in?"

Bo Peabody: "At Village Ventures, we prefer to invest in business models that are tackling mature markets. We'd rather bet on our ability to back the right team that can knock off existing competition than bet on our ability to see around corners. For instance, this is why we invest in vertical publishers in the interactive media space, rather than social media companies."

Word of Caution

One common mistake is the "boil the ocean" business model, where a company claims it will generate revenue in many different ways. I've seen dozens of plans like these, believe it or not. With a straight face, the entrepreneur explains that his or her business will make money from selling ads and sponsorships, selling premium subscriptions, selling market research, and selling merchandise. I've seen angel investors shred entrepreneurs with boil the ocean models simply by asking for a few examples of successful companies that launched using all those types of revenue streams.

Takeaways

- Your business model slide shows how you make money.
- If you have a simple buy low-sell higher model, use this section to lay out the economics of one sale and explain how many units you must sell to cover your overhead.
- If you have a more innovative model, like freemium or exchange, explain it in the simplest way possible.

Learn more at upstartbootcamp.com

Team

It's tough to overemphasize the importance of this topic. Without a strong team, after all, a startup doesn't have much of a chance. Also, most startups are not successful with their initial plan, but a great startup team reacts to what it encounters and adjusts its strategies and tactics.

Here are a few things to consider when drafting the team section of your business plan:

- **Tasks.** What are the primary activities involved in operating your business? Which ones are most critical to the success of the business? Which activities require permanent staffing and which are best handled by consultants or vendors?

- **Roles.** What's the best way to allocate management roles and responsibilities? For example, should there be an inside person (managing operations, product development, customer service, etc.) and an outside person (selling, marketing, landing deals, etc.)?

- **Expertise.** What is the profile of the ideal candidate for each of the management roles? What skills, experience and expertise should each have? What relationships and contacts do they need? To what extent is it important for the candidates to be well-known and regarded within their industries? Which founders have startup experience?

- **Fit.** How well do the current players (i.e. you and your co-founders, if any) fit with the needs you've identified above? This is a tough question to ask about yourself and your potential business partner, but better to do it now than later.

- **Gaps.** Are there key management roles that must be filled? When? Should you hire employees or freelancers? What will it cost to hire them?

- **Advisors.** I often recommend that startups engage two to five advisors[13]—people who can help in critical areas by providing advice and/or introductions. Companies typically grant each advisor 1% or so of their equity with a vesting schedule and specify the advisor's role and time commitment. When picking these people, start by identifying areas of the business where you need additional expertise and/or contacts. Then think of the characteristics of your dream team. Finally, use your personal network to find and engage the right individuals.

- **Order.** If your team is especially strong, consider moving the team slide to the front of your pitch. Strong teams include founders who have built startups and made money for investors, or people who are well known as leaders in their fields.

---

13 Note: An advisor or member of an advisory board is different from a director or member of a board of directors. An advisor plays a less formal role and does not govern the organization, hire / fire the CEO, approve budgets, or represent investors.

Word of Caution

Whether you are looking for a partner, employee, or advisor, don't just reach for the low-hanging fruit, like a friend or personal contact. That could put your company and your relationships at risk. Instead, define the profile of the ideal candidate and then seek out people who meet your criteria.

Once you have suitable answers to these questions it's time to put your selling hat on. Your presentation is a story; tell the tale of who is on your team and why that team is ideally suited to capitalize on the opportunity and strategy you are about to disclose.[14] Here are a few points to include:

- **Genesis.** Explain how you developed the business idea and how your experiences make you particularly knowledgeable about the field—for example, if you learned about the opportunity while working in the industry.

- **Relationships.** Discuss who is on your team and how and when you came together. Just focus on the top management and your advisors for now. Discuss any relevant history. If the team has worked together well enough to want to do it again, for example, be sure to point that out—it's one less risk to worry about.

- **Profiles.** Point out the role each member of the team will play and describe the team members' qualifications. Don't go through long bios. Stick to the most impressive and applicable points. Keep the pace going and do your best to get head nods. You want the internal monologue of those you are pitching to sound something like this: "Yes, that team

---

14 The exception to this rule is if you are pitching to very close friends or family members and you will be the only person on the team.

member sounds like the right woman to run marketing for an internet-based startup."

 # Ask the Expert

Mo Koyfman: "I like to see a team scrappy enough to have built a prototype themselves."

Moshe "Mo" Koyfman is a principal at venture capital firm Spark Capital, where he leads investments in Web services such as www. aviary.com. Prior to joining Spark, Mo spent six years at IAC, most recently as Chief Operating Officer of Connected Ventures, parent of CollegeHumor.com, Vimeo.com and BustedTees.com. Mo is a graduate of The Wharton School and The College of Arts & Sciences at The University of Pennsylvania.

UpStart: "What do you look for in a startup team?"

Mo Koyfman: "A great team is the first thing I look for in an investment opportunity. Successful businesses are built by extremely talented people and that's where my investigation begins. I specifically like to see great co-founders, as there seems to be a unique chemistry that develops with the right mix of leadership at the helm. If technology is an integral part of the product, I also like to see at least one of the founders with a strong technical background. It's certainly ideal if they've had prior success, but not a prerequisite. And it's important that they're still hungry, no matter how successful they've been previously. I also look for a balance between tenacity and passion on the one hand and a willingness to listen and learn on the other, as many mistakes will be made and the company will undoubtedly have to hear their users / customers and pivot over time."

UpStart: "What do you like to hear from a team when they present their business plan?"

Mo Koyfman: "First, I like a business plan to be clear, informative and brief. If your PowerPoint is more than 20 pages, you haven't done a good enough job of crystallizing your plan. In the team section of the plan, I like to know how the team came up with the idea. I tend to prefer ideas hatched from real needs, as opposed to ideas developed in top-down brainstorm sessions. I also like to know how the team knows each other, to get a sense for their shared vision, and to understand how their skills are complementary. I also prefer when teams come with a built product rather than just a plan—particularly for Internet service companies, where it's become easier and cheaper to build basic products right out of the gate. I like to see a team scrappy enough to have built a prototype themselves, with the least amount of money possible."

Reality Check

Who will run the company on a day-to-day basis? Note: This can't be outsourced; it must be a founder, and it will probably be a full-time endeavor, at least after a few months.

_____

How many founders are there? Note: If your answer is one, have you considered joining forces with a partner so you can do more, faster, while reducing the amount you have to pay employees or vendors?

_____

What previous successes and experiences do your founders have that indicate they are qualified to do well with this particular business?

_____

_____

What major gaps are there in the skills and experiences of your founding team?

_____

How and when will you fill the gaps in these skills and experiences?

_____

Do you have an advisory board, set up with formal incentives (e.g. equity options)? If not, what are the profiles of your dream team of advisors?

_____

What employees do you foresee hiring in years one, two and three?

1._____

2._____

3._____

Ask the Expert

Tommy Hilfiger: "Skills and personality traits are more important (to being a great entrepreneur) than background."

Tommy Hilfiger is the founder of Tommy Hilfiger Corporation. An entrepreneur from his earliest days, Tommy skipped college to run a string of retail stores in upstate New York. He later turned down highly sought-after fashion design job offers to start a company of his own. In 1995, Tommy was named Menswear Designer of the Year by the Council of Fashion Designers of America. Three years later Parsons School of Design named him Designer of the Year. By 2004 Tommy Hilfiger Corporation had over 5,000 employees and revenue of more than $1.8 billion. Private investment company Apax Partners acquired the business in 2006.

UpStart: "What does it take to be a great entrepreneur?"

Tommy Hilfiger: "I think skills and personality traits are more important than background. I never went to college or design school, but I had passion, drive, and resourcefulness in droves. When I launched Tommy Hilfiger Corporation, I wasn't trained in the conventional rules of business, but that worked to my advantage. I experimented. I made bold moves. And I adapted as I learned. I credit much of my success to my drive to win and my fear of losing."

UpStart: "To what degree was your team responsible for your success?"

Tommy Hilfiger: "I've always been aware of my strengths and also my weaknesses. Because I acknowledge my weaknesses, I've been able to surround myself with people whose skills complement mine. Building great teams has been essential to my success."

Here's the slide Lee and Amanda present for DigitHeads:

TEAM

Type	Title	Role	Experience
Management	**Lee Richards**	Marketing	ConnectTheDots-Tech Recruiting
	CEO	Finance	AOL-marketing, UCLA-MBA
	Amanda Stevens	Product	ConnectTheDots-Tech Dev.
	CTO	Development	IBM-Tech Dev., U. Mich - Comp Sci
	TBD	Hiring, Training	Call Center management
	VP Operations	Customer Support	Tech customer support
Advisory Board	**Josh Tuttle**	Entrepreneurship	TechJobs - Founder
	Advisor	Advisor	
	Satya Shah	Operations	Geek Squad-Operations
	Advisor	Advisor	

And here's what Lee says while presenting the DigitHeads team slide:

- "I will handle marketing and finance and Amanda will build and update the Web site."

- "We'd like to hire someone to run operations within the next two months."

- "We have two advisors—Josh Tuttle helping with general startup matters and Satya Shah helping with operations."

Takeaways

- Your team is the most important driver of your success as a startup. Most startups don't succeed with the first idea they develop, but a great team can adapt and prevail even after an initial failure.
- If you have holes in the team, don't try to sweep them under the carpet. Address the vacancies and explain what kind of people you'll find to fill them.

Learn more at upstartbootcamp.com

Risk

What are your biggest risks? Maybe there's a chance it could take you longer or cost more than you expect to design and develop your product. Maybe there's a risk that customers won't buy your product at prices that will enable you to generate profits. Perhaps it will cost you too much to market your offerings. Or maybe someone in a garage in Silicon Valley just got a $5 million investment to pursue a similar strategy. There will always be risks. The important thing is to be aware of them and find ways to prevent or cope with them. Here are a few things to consider:

- **Development risk.** If you are developing a new product and going through design, prototyping, testing, etc., you may encounter obstacles that cause delays and/or cost overruns. If you don't build in enough margin for error here, you can run out of cash and then it's "game over."

- **Adoption risk.** If the product or service is very innovative, there's a risk that consumer demand won't be as strong as expected. I learned this lesson the hard way. I once started a company that helped small businesses manage their human resources online. The market research and beta tests went well, but in the end, it turned out that small companies were not ready to store sensitive data online. Being early isn't always a good thing. Some say the pioneers are the ones with the arrows in their backs.

- **Marketing risk.** Even if demand is strong, it may cost you more than expected to accomplish marketing goals, like driving awareness, trial, purchase, or repeat purchase. Media businesses can be tricky in this respect. Let's say you want to start a parenting Web site. Your plan is to create a Web site with content, attract parents to read and contribute to that content, and then sell advertisements to companies that want to reach the parents. The key here is a kind of arbitrage—you have to attract each parent at a low price and then sell access to advertisers at a higher price. If you predict that it will cost an average of $25 per new subscriber, but it actually costs $40, your business could be in for trouble.

- **Competitive risk.** Competition is a tricky subject. There are times when it's good to have competitors; they can reduce risk and cost for a startup by proving that customers will use / pay for the products. But of course, competition can be problematic, too. Rivals can make it tough to close sales, can drive down prices, capture limited resources like employees and distributors, and cause all kinds of other headaches. Competition can also pose a problem with regard to exit strategy. If you are raising money, your investors want a return on their investment. That often comes from a "liquidity event," like being acquired. When a big company looks to gobble up a smaller company, they often look for the one with the most market share, fattest margins, biggest accounts, best technology, and/or fastest growth. You want that to be your company, not your rival's company, or they will be acquired instead of you. When discussing competition, you may want to point out which rivals are likely to be the most troublesome. Be prepared to describe their strengths and weaknesses and their most likely reaction to what you are planning. Will they come after you? Drop prices? Change sales and marketing tactics? You can't know for sure, but it's worth thinking through the next few moves on the chessboard.

 Word of Caution

Some entrepreneurs march into investor meetings and declare that their ventures have no competitors. If that's true, you'd better be absolutely positive. Nothing crushes your credibility like an investor throwing out the name of a direct competitor you didn't know about that just got funded. Also, keep in mind that your audience may have a different perspective than you do about competition; if you want their money, their perspective is what matters. You may not view a particular company as a direct competitor, but your investors might. Be prepared to demonstrate how you are different in ways that are meaningful to customers, not just in your own mind. This is an area where you will get better with every pitch, so be prepared to tweak your slides and comments.

- **Substitution.** Another important consideration is "substitution." Sometimes your biggest competition doesn't come from a competitor at all. Restaurant chains may have lots of competition, but when the economy tanks, people may cook more to save money. Cooking becomes a substitute that steals market share from restaurants.

Once you've identified risks, determine how you'll mitigate them. Can you establish barriers to entry to reduce competition? Barriers to entry are defense mechanisms, like patents, long-term exclusive contracts with customers or distribution partners, or strong brands. Coca-Cola is a classic example. They sell sugar water, more or less. It's probably not that tough to come up with a new sugar water drink, but try to bring your new drink to market and you'll learn a painful lesson about barriers to entry. Coca-Cola has forged exclusive relationships with distributors, retailers, and restaurants. They've also spent 100 years building one of the most well-known and well-regarded brand names on Earth, so customers all over the world ask for the product.

 Reality Check

When you think of what could go wrong with your startup, what are the top three things that keep you awake at night?

1._____

2._____

3._____

Every company faces competition in some form or another, even if that competition comes from products or services that serve as substitutes. What are the three biggest sources of competition, and how well are they doing?

1._____

2._____

3._____

What companies don't compete directly with yours now, but could conceivably enter your market and pose a threat?

_____

What are the top three steps you can take to mitigate risk and preempt competition?

1._____

2._____

3._____

Here's the slide Lee and Amanda show for DigitHeads:

RISK

COMPETITION

	Digit Heads	Geek Squad	Live Person
Remote tech support	✔	✔	✔
Low monthly fee	✔		
Tailored to needs of people 40+	✔		

Primary Risks:
- Will customers over 45 find the concept appealing enough to pay?
- Can we acquire customers at a low enough cost?

Lee's comments:

- "GeekSquad and LivePerson offer remote tech support, as do many independent techies. We're different because we offer a low monthly fee and tailor our offerings to the 45+ set."

- "One big risk we face is whether our service will be adopted by the market. We're taking a phased approach with flexibility built in, so that we can adjust our positioning and pricing if necessary."

- "Another risk is customer acquisition cost. We'll do extensive testing to figure out the best combination of message and media."

Lee also prepares a backup slide, just in case his audience wants more information about how DigitHeads is differentiated from specific competitors. That way, he'll be prepared if he gets any tough questions.

Takeaways

- When you think about what could go wrong with your business, what keeps you up at night?
- Think about your business as if you are playing chess. Describe the risks and threats you anticipate and show how you will preempt and react to them.
- Be prepared to show how you are clearly differentiated from your competition.

Learn more at upstartbootcamp.com

Progress

When you show your business plan to a potential investor, advisor or partner, you can be sure they'll ask themselves one question: "Will this venture succeed?" The single best way to prove your venture will succeed is by showing that it's *already* working. A common term for describing this is "traction."

What can you show in this part of your business plan to demonstrate that you've made progress in important areas—areas that are strong predictors of your ultimate success? Here are a few ideas:

- **Team.** How close are you to having the team you'll ultimately need to execute the next phases of your plan? To demonstrate traction, show that you have secured key players on that team, including advisory board members.

- **Product.** Product development can be risky. It can take longer or cost more than you expect. If you have a prototype, beta, or market-ready version of your product, make that clear in your plan.

- **Paying customers.** One of the best signs of progress is to show that customers are willing to buy your products. If you can show that, by all means do it here. If not, at least try to show that customers will use your product for free, as with a free trial or beta test.

- **Marketing.** If you are interacting directly with customers, you'll need to prove that the lifetime value of your customers exceeds your cost of acquiring those customers. Early test-marketing campaigns can be helpful in this regard. For example, you can do a quick, inexpensive "search engine marketing" (SEM) test by purchasing keywords on Google and tracking your results.

- **Deals.** Having signed agreements with partner companies (e.g. distribution partners, retailers) is a great way to show progress. Having data to show that those deals are driving measurable results is even better. If you can't get a signed agreement, or activate a partnership, try to get a letter of intent showing that a company is willing to partner with you once certain conditions are met.

Many entrepreneurs get frustrated with this notion. "How am I supposed to show progress when I haven't raised any money yet—that's what I need the money *for?*" they ask. The answer is called bootstrapping.

While the term bootstrapping dates back to the 1800s, the concept couldn't be more timely. In the late 1990s when I launched my first venture, the first thing most entrepreneurs did as was raise capital. Then you developed your product and proved you could sell it. It was all backward. And for most of us, it's ancient history. The new rules are: build a great team, develop your product, prove customers will use or buy it, and *then* raise capital if necessary. That's how companies like Apple, YouTube, Facebook, Liz Lange, Stila, Yahoo and Google did it.

There are several advantages to bootstrapping:

- **Speed.** Raising capital can take a long time, and it's pretty much a full-time job. Good bootstrappers spend that time building teams, developing products, and generating revenue instead. Before you head out to seek funding, think about what you need the money for. One of my clients—Jeff—recently told me he needed to raise capital so he could hire employees to help him with marketing and sales. At the time the economy was in particularly bad shape. I told Jeff he'd probably have to spend six months raising the capital and thousands on legal fees to close the round—if he could raise the money at all, given the environment, and the fact that his business had made very little progress to date. I challenged him to consider whether it was really worth waiting the six months. Why not find hungry, entrepreneurial talent, give them some equity, help them find a side-gig to pay the rent, and get started building the business *today* instead of a half-year later?

- **Flexibility.** Once you've raised money by convincing investors "Plan A" will work, it can be difficult and time consuming to get those investors to embrace "Plan B." Typically, bootstrapped businesses can change direction more quickly.

- **Efficiency.** If you don't have it, you can't spend it. During the dot-com bubble in the late 1990s, money-losing startups wasted millions on Superbowl ads, game rooms, and in-house chefs. Bootstrappers tend to use their money in a more disciplined manner, tracking expenses carefully and spending only on the most efficient tactics.

- **Capital preservation.** As a rule of thumb, when you raise a lot of money for an early-stage company, you give up a lot of ownership, or equity. In some cases, especially when factoring in risk, a founder can make more money owning 100% of a small but profitable bootstrapped business, than owning 10% of a company backed with millions in venture capital. Also, note that you can bootstrap part of the way toward your goals and then raise capital. That way, you'll have more progress under your belt and will be able to raise money at a higher valuation, giving up less equity per dollar invested.

So, how exactly *do* you bootstrap? Here are a few techniques:

- **Build on the backs of clients.** Instead of reaching out to investors for financing, land a customer willing to pay some or all fees up-front. Use the cash from the fees to cover operating expenses, and repeat.

- **Ham-and-egg.** Microsoft is one of the largest companies around, but it didn't start that way. Bill Gates was actually a master bootstrapper before he made all those billions. He approached the then-mighty IBM and sold them a software platform to go on their new personal computers. Thing is, he didn't actually have the software platform, but he found someone who *had* built one and got that person to sell it to him for $50,000. Only catch was, Gates didn't have the money. So, he convinced IBM to give him an advance of $50,000, used the money to buy the software, and sold it to IBM as MS-DOS. Working both sides of a deal that way is often called "ham-and-egging."[15]

- **Moonlight.** During the early days of a bootstrapped startup, most founders can't pay themselves much. Many take part-time or consulting work to pay the bills and maintain interaction with the world beyond their startup.

- **Phasing.** Break daunting challenges down into manageable parts. Set short-term goals that you can accomplish without breaking the bank and stay laser-focused on reaching them.

- **Barter.** Instead of buying something, look for ways to trade your products or services. Media companies do this all the time. A magazine, newspaper or Web site might give Dell a free advertisement in exchange for some laptops, for example.

- **Equity.** Hiring a great chief marketing officer will probably cost. If that's just not feasible for you financially and you

---

15 Depending on when you read this, Bill Gates may or may not still be the world's richest person, with a net worth of around $40 billion.

need that great CMO yesterday, you may consider offering equity in the company in exchange for a lower salary. If at all possible, negotiate a vesting schedule with the person, so the equity will be earned over time.

- **Team-up.** On a related note, it's generally easier to get more done with less startup capital if you launch a business with multiple founders. With multiple founders, you have a bigger network of contacts for business and financial leads, more people to roll up their sleeves and get early results without needing to get paid, and less chance that all the founders will be overcome by fear at any given time.

 ## Ask the Expert

Liz Lange: "Nobody has more passion about their work than a founder."

Liz Lange launched her eponymous line of fashionable maternity clothing in 1997. Within eight years, the company grew to over $10 million in revenues, secured partnerships with Target and Nike, and established a cult following said to include the likes of Cindy Crawford, Gwyneth Paltrow and Kate Winslet. In the process she changed the way women, retailers and the media think about maternity wear, despite the fact that industry experts told her it would never work. Liz Lange also bootstrapped her way to success. Here's how she did it:

UpStart: "How did you build a multi-million dollar brand with limited startup capital?"

Liz Lange: "I started with no money and eventually borrowed $50,000. Initially, I did everything myself. I waited on every customer. I packed the FedEx boxes. I was the fit model. I did my own PR by calling editors to write about my business. To avoid getting stuck with unsold inventory, I produced all my clothing to order. And before opening a retail store, I just had a small office where customers could see me by appointment."

UpStart: "Did you find that there were advantages to bootstrapping the way you did?"

Liz Lange: "Starting with limited capital helped me become successful. In the end, let's face it, most businesses are thrift businesses, even the supposedly glamorous ones. Starting with less taught me to operate the business efficiently, and those lessons stayed with me throughout good times and bad."

"I had to be very smart about what I did and didn't spend on, and that led me to make smart decisions. I also had to focus on the bottom line from the very beginning, as opposed to startups that raise a lot of capital and tend to lose sight of the bottom line in favor of generating revenue."

"Since I had to do almost everything myself, I understood every aspect of my business and got direct feedback about the needs of my customers. Even after I could afford to delegate, I made it a point to interact with customers personally, even if only via e-mail, as I had learned the value of staying connected to them. Plus, doing everything myself ensured that everything was done well. Nobody has more passion about their work than a founder. It's your baby, after all."

Reality Check

Give yourself a grade of A, B, or C in terms of your progress in the following areas.

Team in place: (circle one)   A   B   C

Product developed: (circle one)   A   B   C

Demand proven: (circle one)   A   B   C

Revenue generated: (circle one)   A   B   C

What are the top three accomplishments your business has made to date that demonstrate your ability to succeed?

1._____

2._____

3._____

Pretend for a moment that *you* are the investor, and a founder is pitching you an opportunity to invest in what is actually your startup. What milestones would you want to see the company hit before writing a check?

1._____

2._____

3._____

How can you make more progress toward your goals before you raise money?

_____

_____

_____

_____

Here's the DigitHeads slide on progress:

PROGRESS

- **Product.** Beta site operational

- **Demand.** 1,000 survey responses - most favorable

- **Marketing.** 5% of visitors want to be notified when we're live

---

Lee and Amanda make the following comments when showing this slide:

- "We have a beta version of our Web site and call center up and running."

- "We did extensive research, including over 1,000 surveys; over 50% of respondents said they'd pay $10 per month."

- "So far, 5% of people coming to the beta site submitted their e-mail addresses and asked us to let them join when they can subscribe."

More resources:

Bootstrap Finance: The Art of Start-Ups, by Amar Bhide[16]. Bhide was my first professor of entrepreneurship and had a profound impact on me, as did this article. The vast majority of startups launch with very limited funding. As Bhide explains, bootstrappers often start with a copycat idea in a niche market, rather than with some big unproven idea. They find ways to generate cash early,

---

16 Harvard Business Review, November 1992.

peddle expensive products or services via direct personal selling, and concentrate on cash flow above all else.

Takeaways

- The single best way to prove your venture will succeed is by showing that it's already working.
- Instead of raising capital and then making progress, look for ways to bootstrap—to get traction toward your goals before or even instead of raising capital.

Learn more at upstartbootcamp.com

Implementation

In real estate, the three most important factors are "location, location, and location," At startups, the corresponding factors are execution, execution, and execution. As with many complex problems, it's easier to tackle the challenges of execution after breaking them down into smaller parts. Taking a phased approach makes execution a bit less daunting; it also helps to reduce risk, because after each phase you can step back, measure your performance, and decide whether to move on to the next one. Without stopping to do that periodically, it's easy to find yourself in a position where you've thrown good money (and time) after bad.

For each phase of execution, it's helpful to consider the following:

- **Timing.** How long should it take to plan, execute and analyze each phase? Which phases can be tested simultaneously and which need to follow one another?

- **Tasks.** What are the essential activities you'll execute in each phase?

- **Goals.** What are the key objectives for each phase? For example, maybe you want to prove you can develop a new product on time, hire your team without going over budget, or land enough new customers to convince yourself that there's sufficient demand for your service.

- **Metrics.** How will you measure performance? What targets should you set to determine whether to move forward after each phase? Setting targets helps you take an objective view, instead of letting your emotions get the best of you.

 ## Reality Check

What are the most important milestones your company will hit during the next four calendar quarters?

Months 1 - 3: _____

Months 4 - 6: _____

Months 7 – 9: _____

Months 10 - 12: _____

What metrics will be most helpful in measuring your company's performance over the next year (e.g. number of customers, revenue, acquisition cost per customer)?

1._____

2._____

3._____

What accomplishments will have the most profound impact on your business? For example: reaching a critical mass of visitors to a Web site, so you can start selling advertising, or hitting targets set by a retailer that is testing your products, so they will agree to roll out distribution to more stores.

_____

_____

_____

Here's the slide Lee and Amanda use for implementation:

IMPLEMENTATION

Months	Goals	Tasks	Metrics
1 - 3	Fill gaps in team Test operations on limited scale	Hire VP Operations, 3 tech support reps Service over 500 customers per month	Customer satisfaction rates
4 - 7	Test marketing tactics	Run keyword buys Launch PR campaign Start influencer give-away program	Cost to acquire visitors Conversion of visitors to paid subscribers
8 - 12	Ramp up revenue	Implement AARP promotions	Revenue per month

Here's what Lee says while showing this slide to prospective investors:

- "Over the next three months we'll build out our core team and test our operations, to make sure we're prepared for customers once we start marketing."

- "Then, we'll test our different marketing approaches and measure the results to figure out what's most cost-effective."

- "For the rest of the year, we'll invest in the marketing tactics that work best and start our partnership with AARP. During this phase, we'll start to generate significant monthly revenue."

> ## Takeaways
>
> - Success is all about execution, so a business plan should include a roadmap for how the founders expect to execute in the near-term.
> - Breaking challenges down into phases makes them easier to tackle. Each phase should be tied to deadlines, goals, tasks, and metrics.

Learn more at upstartbootcamp.com

Projections

Financial projections for startups involve a bit of irony.

On one hand, the numbers are almost always wrong. After all, it's tough enough to predict sales or earnings at a company that's been operating for 30 years—think of the armies of analysts and investors who try in vain to predict the earnings of a stock like Apple every quarter. Now consider that a startup has little to no operating history and may very well be attempting something that hasn't been done before. Good luck predicting five years of revenues and expenses.

On the other hand, the numbers are essential. They tie together the assumptions and goals you've created throughout the rest of your plan, forming a quantitative roadmap for your business. That's important, whether or not you plan to raise capital.

Here are some things to consider when running your projections:

What you'll need. You'll include just one or two financial charts in your business plan pitch, but to create those charts you'll need a financial model with more detail. That model typically consists of several Excel worksheets linked to each other—five-year statements of profits and loss (P&L), cash flow statements, and balance sheets. Depending on your business, you may also want to build separate but linked worksheets showing how your team builds over time and how your customers and accounts grow.

If your heart is palpitating at the very thought of crunching these numbers, you are not alone. If you have limited expertise in finance, accounting, and Excel you should get help (UpStart Bootcamp has classes and coaches available). However, as with the rest of the business plan, be sure you understand the mechanics of the numbers, even if you have someone else do the heavy lifting.

 Word of Caution

Many entrepreneurs without a financial background get help from friends in finance. Sometimes these friends create models so complicated that the entrepreneurs never fully understand how they function and have trouble explaining them to investors and/ or modifying them. Make sure you understand your own financial model, even if it means taking time to learn / brush up on your Excel skills.

How to develop your projections. Whether you build the model yourself or get assistance, follow this simple rule: build from the bottom up and validate from the top down.

Building from the bottom up means starting with the details of each driver of cost and revenue and extrapolating from there. Top down means looking at the overall market and making assumptions about how your company will fit in. For example, let's say you are projecting sales for a widget company (Widget Co.). Maybe you plan to have five salespeople or reps during January of 2011. How many calls can each rep make per day? Per week? Per month? What percentage of calls lead to a sale? How much revenue does an average sale generate? Looking at what one person can accomplish in one day keeps you focused on what drives your numbers. Here's an example:

BOTTOM-UP CALCULATION: WIDGET CO. SALES REVENUE, JANUARY 2011	
Number of sales reps	5
Sales calls per rep	40/day x 5 days/week x 4 weeks = 800 calls/month
Percent of calls that generate sales	15%
# of sales closed per month	120
Average product price	$100
Average # products sold per transaction	5
Average transaction size	$500
Sales revenue per month	120 transactions x $500 per sale = $60,000

 Word of Caution

Presenting your financials to potential investors can be tricky. If you put a chart full of numbers in front of a savvy investor and pause, the investor will find ways to shoot holes in your numbers. That can impact your confidence right before you ask for their money. Not good. I recommend that founders take this bull by the horns. Lead investors through the discussion. Don't leave long pauses. Preempt questions by explaining that you built your model the right way and by pointing out key takeaways (see discussion of "which numbers are important" below).

Once you've built your projections from the bottom-up, step back and look at the big picture—a top-down view. Are the projections realistic from that perspective? Let's assume that after five years of growth, your widget company is really cooking, on paper. Your bottom-up numbers show a large team of sales reps moving thousands of units per month. You have enough people to do what you are projecting, in theory, but will the market support the level of sales? Let's say your total addressable market accounts for $100 million in revenue now, and you expect it to grow 5% per year, so it will be nearly $130 million in five years. After half a decade, your bottom-up projections show you generating $25 million per year. That's a market share of nearly 20 percent. Is that realistic? If not, sharpen your pencil and limit revenue growth in later years.

Which numbers are most important? A financial model contains hundreds of numbers and formulae and dozens of assumptions. Here are a few that matter most:

- **Break-even.** Have a prediction for when your business will reach break-even, or reach profitability, on a monthly basis. That's when cash stops flowing out and starts flowing in. Before that point, your company will operate at a loss and eat into its startup capital (the amount of loss per month is also called a "burn rate"). Also, predict how many units you'll need to sell per month in order to break even, so you'll have a sales target to shoot for.

- **Scale.** Have a ballpark prediction for what your annual revenue will be after five years. You'll never get the number right, but you should be able to predict the order of magnitude (e.g. are you shooting for sales of $1 million? $10 million? $100 million?) That will be help investors, partners, and other stakeholders grasp the size of your opportunity and help them to know that if things go well, the rewards will be worth the risks.

- **Capital requirements.** Have a prediction for the amount of investment capital that will be required to get the company through the next five years. Raising capital is difficult and time-consuming, so you should avoid any surprises on this front. Also, future rounds of funding can dilute[17] existing

---

17 Dilution is the degree to which a shareholder's ownership

shareowners, so you'll want to manage expectations and be sure that you won't be giving away so much equity that the venture is no longer worth your while.

- **Balance.** Make sure you are being realistic about the way revenues and expenses grow in relation to one another. Sometimes entrepreneurs predict "hockey stick" revenue growth[18], but fail to take into account that certain expenses, like customer service, tend to grow in-step with revenue.

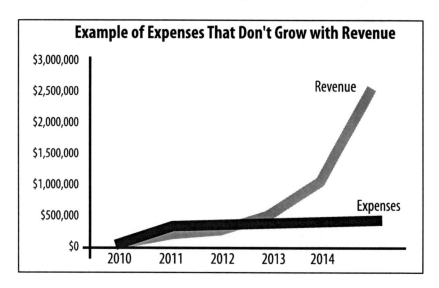

- **Key assumptions.** You'll base your projections on many assumptions. Be aware of which ones, when modified slightly, change your projections dramatically (e.g. the cost of acquiring an average customer or the amount of revenue generated by an average transaction). Also, know which assumptions are common to your industry and make sure

---

percentage is reduced by future issues of equity, such as when a company sells more stock or grants stock to employees.

18 Growth that, when plotted on a chart, starts out nearly horizontal and suddenly spikes upward.

your numbers are in line with standards (e.g. those might include markups, or sales per square foot in retail).

- **Use of proceeds.** If you raise money, understand how you plan to spend it, broken down by expense category (e.g. staffing, marketing, rent, etc.).

- **Comparables.** Be aware of companies similar to yours and how they've fared in terms of issues like break-even, scale, and capital requirements. By doing your homework, you'll have more confidence in the accuracy of your projections and you'll be in a better position to pitch them. Here are a few examples of when it's great to have some comparables:

Comparables For Financial Projections	
Assumption / Metric	**Reality Check**
It will take six months to develop our Web site, using an outsourced vendor, at a cost of $200,000.	We have bids from three vendors who have built similar Web sites and they are all safely within that range. We verified these numbers with their client references.
On average, it will take us 60 days to close a sale.	According to our advisors, our two competitors had sales cycles of about 60 days at our stage of development.
The average customer will renew his or her subscription for 180 days.	This is an industry standard, as reported by ABC Industry Association.
Our margins will increase over time, because our revenue will grow faster than our expenses. At the end of year five, we'll have margins of 40 percent.	These margins are in line with the numbers in our competitor's annual report for their fifth year of operation.
We will reach sales of $10 million by the end of year three, which will give us about a two percent market share.	Our closest competitor hit sales of $10 million after three years of operation.

Before we turn back to our fictitious friends at DigitHeads, one word of caution:

 Word of Caution

Whatever you do, DON'T utter the following words to your prospective investors: "Our financials are conservative." It's a dead giveaway that you are a rookie. Of course they are not conservative! In fact, they are wildly optimistic.

Reality Check

Did you build your financials on a bottom-up basis, by projecting financial activities month by month?

How much investment capital will it take to get your company through the next five years?

During what quarter (three-month window) do you expect to reach profitability?

What level of sales do you need to hit in order to reach profitability?

How much revenue do you expect to generate during your fifth year?

What's your pre-tax profit divided by your revenue during your fifth year (AKA "profit margin")?

How can you demonstrate that your financial projections are within the realm of reasonability? For example, can you point to other companies that reached similar levels of growth using the same amount of resources within the time frame you are projecting?

Here's the slide Lee and Amanda present[19]:

PROJECTIONS

DIGITHEADS P&L		YEAR 1		YEAR 2		YEAR 3
Revenue						
New customers		2,075		16,790		20,149
Customer defections		379		3,797		4,556
Total customers		1,696		14,690		26,229
Subscription revenue		92,292		881,834		2,561,514
UpSell revenue		46,355		442,911		1,286,550
Total revenue		138,646		1,324,745	$	3,848,064
Expenses						
Tech development		45,000	$	150,000	$	187,500
Team		325,000	$	600,000	$	750,000
Marketing	$	155,625	$	1,300,000	$	1,600,000
Rent	$	14,000	$	120,000	$	150,000
Legal, acctg, consulting	$	9,000	$	50,000	$	60,000
Supplies, misc	$	5,000	$	20,000	$	25,000
Total Expenses	$	553,625	$	2,240,000	$	2,772,500
Pretax profit	$	(414,979)	$	(915,255)	$	1,075,564

Lee's comments when presenting this slide:

- "We built our financial model from the bottom up and compared the annual numbers to those of a few similar companies as a reality check. We'll be happy to send you the model so you can go through the assumptions."

- "We think we'll need about $2M in total investment capital, starting with $500K for the next 12 months."

- "We anticipate breaking even in the middle of year two, with about 10,000 subscribers."

---

19 We typically recommend five year projections, but limited our example to three years to make it easier to read given the format of this book.

More resources:

Hire an expert coach to help you develop your financial projections at upstartbootcamp.com/coaching

---

Takeaways

- Build your financials from the bottom up, and use top-down numbers for a reality check.
- If you need help running the numbers, that's fine, but keep things simple and be sure you understand how the formulae and assumptions work, because you may have to modify them yourself or field tough questions from investors.
- Key analyses include: Break-even volume and timing, revenue scalability, capital requirements, use of proceeds, and comparables.

Learn more at upstartbootcamp.com

Financing

This is the last slide in your business plan, answering the all-important questions: "How much money do we need to build this business (or the next phase of it)?" and "How and when will owners get a return on their investment?" You'll want these answers even if you don't plan to raise outside financing.

How much money do you need? If you can get through to break-even within 12 to 18 months, you'll probably want to raise enough to get there, plus a buffer in case things don't go as planned (and they won't).

If you'll be facing several years of losses, a good rule of thumb is to raise capital for the next 12 months, plus a buffer. Some entrepreneurs are tempted to bring in all of the money they'll need for the lifetime of their business up-front. Their rationale goes something like this: "Fundraising is difficult and time consuming, so why do it more than once?" Here's why:

First, it's tougher to attract a lot of investment capital at an early stage, since you have less progress to show; you may not be able to get the money, or it may take you a very long time to get it. Second, you'll give up more equity if you raise a lot of money early on. That's because when you're just starting out, your company is worth less—it has a low valuation. If things go well, your company will be worth more as you get additional traction. So, you can raise some capital now at a low valuation, and raise more capital in the future, at a higher valuation, selling a smaller amount of your equity.

How will owners get a return on their investment? As a founder, you'll want to make sure you are rewarded for all your hard work. Investors put in capital, and they'll want a way to pull significantly more capital out.

If you are pitching to investors, tell them why you believe (not promise) they'll make a profit on their investment. If that strategy is to create something valuable and sell it to a larger company, explain precisely what you need to build and who is most likely to buy it. A good way to do this is to look at recent acquisition activity in related markets. Be sure to consider *why* companies made acquisitions. Were they looking to buy a talented management team? A hot, up-and-coming brand? A relationship with customers or distributors? Advanced technology?

Also, look at how the acquiring companies valued their target.[20] Their method of valuation will help you predict what your company might be worth. Financial buyers might have bought a company for a price equal to some multiple of cash flow or profit—eight times earnings, for example. Big companies with efficient sales and marketing processes might see a small company differently. Maybe the small company is growing sales very quickly, but is barely eking out a profit. The big company might focus on some multiple of sales such as two times sales, because they know they can boost profits when they increase efficiencies. Finally, see whether major milestones seem to be required for acquisition. Maybe in your industry, the last few companies that were bought had recently hit $10 million in sales. That could be a magic number you'll need to reach before companies consider buying you.

---

20 This information can be tricky to find. Sometimes press releases announcing M&A deals list prices paid and the financial performance of the target company. If public companies are involved, similar information may be listed in their SEC filing. Otherwise, you may need to speak to industry insiders.

Reality Check

Are you trying to raise money? If so, how much?

_____

What will you use the money for?

_____

_____

What milestones will the money enable you to hit?

_____

_____

What happens when you hit those milestones? Will you need more money? If so, how much?

_____

_____

What are your proposed terms for raising the money? What's the rationale behind those terms?

_____

_____

_____

If all goes well, how—and to what extent—will your investors pull out profits?

_____

_____

Here's the DigitHeads slide on funding:

FINANCING

- Seeking $500K
- Will fund operations for 12 months
- After that, $1.5 - $3M required to reach profitability
- Within 5 years, the company expects to be an attractive
  acquisition candidate for companies such as AARP, Amazon, or WalMart

Brand	Year Sold	Acquirer	Price	Sales	Multiple on Sales
Support Tech	2009	Dell	$80M	$11M	7x
PC Fix	2008	Tesco	$120M	$15M	8x

Lee's comments:

- "We're looking to raise $500K now, which will get us through the next 12 months."

- "After that we'll need another round, which will get us through to profitability and will position us to be acquired after five years."

- "Based on the comparable transactions in this chart, if we hit our revenue projections we could be worth more than $70 M."

At this point, Lee and Amanda ask their potential investors if they're interested. They spark a dialogue that continues for the rest of the meeting and beyond.

Takeaways

- In this final part of the business plan, you'll address two questions: "How much money do we need to build this business (or the next phase of it)?" and "What's the potential return on investment for investors and for founders earning sweat equity?" You'll want to answer those questions whether or not you are raising outside capital.
- Instead of building your business and hoping for the best, use this part of the plan to craft a reasonable exit strategy.

Backup Slides

A presentation is like a new business—it's very difficult to predict what will happen. In order to succeed you must be able to adjust your pitch as you go. Backup slides make that easier. With backup slides, you can keep your pitch length to about 15 slides, but have the flexibility to pull out additional slides if you need them—such as:

- When you are asked a particularly tough question, or if an audience member disagrees with one of your points. You'll want to be prepared with a strong, clear answer, and it's always easier to wheel out a backup slide than try to make up an answer on the fly.

- When you are asked for more detail. For example, you might show your annual totals in your financial projections, but an investor may want to see monthly numbers. In that case, it's great to have the data ready on a backup slide.

You can develop some backup slides before you start to get feedback, by guessing which issues audience members *may* have questions about. You'll also identify opportunities to create backup slides as you begin to pitch. Every time you give a presentation, you'll learn something that can make the pitch better the next time. And if you build good backup slides, you'll be able to respond to audience concerns or questions with clear, concise answers and minimal stress. Here are a few topics your backup slides may cover:

- Market research results
- Feedback from initial customers
- Press clippings
- Profiles of key competitors
- Primary operations of the business
- Organizational charts
- Job descriptions for key hires
- Resumes of employees
- List of prospective partners, suppliers, distributors, and/or customers
- Access to closed beta sites or prototypes
- Profiles of comparable companies that support your contentions
- Letters of intent from major accounts

Takeaways

- Backup slides are great when you want to be prepared for tough questions without modifying your core presentation.
- Consider adding a backup slide after each time an investor or advisor brings up a point you haven't fleshed out in your pitch.

Learn more at upstartbootcamp.com

Part Three:
Your Pitch In Action

This final part of the book will explain how to use your business plan materials to secure meetings and deliver your pitch. You'll learn about the typical process to follow if you are raising capital and some common mistakes to avoid.

CHAPTER 10

Putting The Pieces Together

Once you have your pitch deck and financial projections in order, you'll need a few more documents. But don't despair—you've done the heavy lifting, so the rest will be easy. Here's what you need and how you'll put the pieces together.

Elevator Pitch. As you look for advice, investors, business partners, customers, etc., you'll be networking a lot—both online and offline. You'll reach out to your close contacts, of course. But you'll also want them to reach out to *their* contacts on your behalf, so you'll need to explain your story in a way that's easy for them to grasp and pass along to others. The key to making this work is to have a great elevator pitch. To make it great, you must be able to communicate the essence of your venture in a way that's clear, fast, and compelling. The bad news is that this is much tougher than it seems. The good news is that you have a head start, thanks to the work you did crafting your strategy. Remember the WordPlay exercise? Take your answer, wordsmith it so it sounds good when spoken, and you'll have created your elevator pitch.

You may want two versions of that elevator pitch. Let's say you run into a classmate from school at a party or conference. As you catch up, you'll invariably get the question "So, what are you up to these days?" That's the perfect segue to the short version of your elevator pitch:

"I'm launching WingNut Marketing. We're a marketing agency that helps WingNut producers boost their sales online."

Even if you get interrupted at this point, your classmate knows what you are doing, and can keep you in mind for potential introductions. Have more time? Add critical details:

"I used to run the leading WingNut manufacturing company and I figured out some really effective ways to market online."

"There are more 1,000 WingNut producers and most of them don't know how to boost sales through online marketing."

"We're the first agency with a focus on Internet marketing for WingNut producers."

Now your classmate knows there's a big problem out there and that you have a unique way of solving it, with a clear benefit to the customer. He also know you have credibility because of your background. If you think your classmate may have valuable contacts, you can add "keep me in mind if you run into any (fill in the blank — WingNut producers, investors, WingNut marketers, etc.)."

Practice this pitch out loud again and again, until you can recite it in your sleep. Even when someone catches you off-guard, or after you've had a few cocktails at an event or dinner, you must be able to deliver your elevator pitch perfectly. Write it on a Post-it and stick it on your wall so you can fire it off when a potential customer, investor, partner, or member or the press calls unexpectedly.

You'll probably use your elevator pitch proactively, as well. Once you know what you need, go through your contacts[21] and put them into categories based on how they could potentially be of assistance. Maybe some could give you useful feedback, others

---

21 I do this with Microsoft Outlook. I add keywords to the notes sections of each person's v-card, like "angel investor," "venture capital," or "startup lawyer." When it's time to network, I can search by these keywords. I also use LinkedIn and Facebook extensively for networking.

could help generate sales leads, and still another group could lead to investors. Reach out to them with a very, very short email—something like this:

Jeff,

I hope all is well. As a reminder, we sat on a panel together last year at the American Marketing Association convention in Tampa. I'm launching WingNut Marketing. We're a marketing agency that helps WingNut producers boost their sales online. I know you've done some angel investing in the space, and I'd like to see what you think of my concept. Are you available to meet for a coffee sometime in the next few weeks? If so, I'll send you a one-page synopsis of the venture.

Regards,

John Sparks

www.newco.com

One-page synopsis (AKA "one-pager"). Once you find a contact who has heard / read your elevator pitch and expressed interest in learning more about your new business, it's time to introduce the one-pager.

The one-pager is a brief synopsis of your business plan pitch deck. It's designed with one very specific purpose: to get someone interested in taking a meeting with you (see warning below—don't send your pitch ahead of time). Don't try to jam everything from the pitch deck onto one page. Instead, think of it as a teaser—a sales document to whet the appetite of your audience and leave them wanting more.

To create your one-pager, start with your pitch deck outline. Ignore the Implementation, Competition, and Financials slides; you'll explain those in person. Summarize the other slides using short, pithy sentences that are easy to read and headlines to provide a clear roadmap. See the DigitHeads sample one-pager below as an example. When you are finished, save the one-pager as a PDF. That way, when you send it via email your recipients will see it the way you created it, no matter what kind of software they are using.

Word of Caution

Don't send your deck ahead of time, if at all possible. The deck is meant to be a presentation. When you are delivering it in person, your deck is a powerful tool for convincing your audience that you have a good team, idea, and approach. It's intentionally minimalist, so your audience will concentrate on you and the words you speak. It's not designed as a standalone document. Without you there, it won't have nearly the same persuasive impact. Also, when you pitch it, you are there to address any doubts or confusion immediately. Without you there, doubts can be amplified and confusion can turn to frustration.

digitheads

DigitHeads provides remote tech support for people over 45. They can call DigitHeads at any time, with any tech-related question or issue, and get help from well-informed, well-spoken tech experts.

OPPORTUNITY

People over 45 are sometimes called digital immigrants because they didn't learn technology while still in school – they had to learn it later in life to keep up with kids and colleagues. Now they're surrounded by it, from computers, smartphones, and digital cameras, to ipods, DVRs, and web sites. They grew up reading the instructions, and calling for help. But today's tech is more DIY-oriented, and support is more automated. The average tech support call takes 45 minutes and over 60% do not resolve problems. That frustrates digital immigrants. Together, they make up a large, growing market. 25 million Americans over 45 place 125 million calls per year to manufacturer tech support, and the numbers are growing by 10% per year.

THE DIGITHEADS APPROACH

DigitHeads acts as a tech support concierge for digital immigrants, providing live, remote help with basic tech challenges across all products and services. DigitHeads caters to the specialized needs of its, by doing away with long hold times, confusing automated phone systems, and service reps with thick accents.

BUSINESS MODEL

Customers pay $9.95 per month for basic services, and a $125 up-charge for premium services like help setting up wireless networks or removing viruses. Management anticipates that it will spend $75 to acquire an average customer, and that lifetime margin per customer will be $225.

TEAM

Lee Richards is CEO. Lee previously founded, ran, and sold a tech job site, ConnectTheDots. Before that, he ran marketing for a division of AOL. Amanda Stevens is CTO. She served as CTO of ConnectTheDot, where she worked closely with Lee. Amanda previously ran tech development for a consumer-facing unit of IBM. The company has two advisors. Josh Tuttle founded TechJobs, and will help with general startup matters. Satya Shah ran operations for GeekSquad, and will help with operations.

FUNDING

DigitHeads is raising a $500K seed round. Proceeds will be used to fund operations for 12 months, during which the company expects to surpass $100,000 in revenue. At that point, DigitHeads will raise additional capital that will enable the company to reach profitability, and grow rapidly.

To learn more, please contact LeeRichards@DigitHeads.com.

Non-disclosure agreement (NDA). An NDA is a legal agreement designed to prevent your documents from getting into the wrong hands (e.g. being passed along to competitors). Unfortunately, many inexperienced entrepreneurs misuse NDAs. When approaching venture capitalists, angel networks, or seasoned angels, I recommend holding off on NDAs until after you've made an initial presentation. Why?

- Building a successful startup is about 95% execution and about 5% idea, which you'll probably change as you go. If all you have is the idea and not the ability to execute, you have bigger problems than NDAs.

- You are probably asking your audience for a favor, like considering an investment in your company or giving you advice. Asking them to sign an NDA can be seen as a slap in the face to someone who is about to do you a favor.

- Some investors will view your request to have them sign an NDA as a sign of naiveté. Others, like venture capitalists, may refuse to sign an NDA early in the pitch process as a policy.

There are a few exceptions. It's fine to ask service providers you've hired (lawyers, accountants, Web developers, PR firms, etc.) to sign NDAs. If you are pitching to another entrepreneur or someone else capable of and potentially interested in pursuing your idea and you don't have a close relationship or connection with that person, it is better to be safe than sorry and request that he or she sign an NDA. If you've come up with some sort of truly radical innovation, you might want to insist on an NDA, but be realistic about what constitutes a radical innovation. Finally, it's perfectly reasonable to request an NDA before sharing due diligence documents (see below).

Due diligence documents. This is material that lets an investor learn more about you, your concept, and your progress to-date. There are no standards for what this contains or how it is presented, but it might include things like market research, customer lists, access to prototypes, profiles of your competitors, your financial model, resumes of team members, contracts with customers or suppliers, etc. Sophisticated investors will often provide a due diligence list for you to follow. Get an NDA signed before sharing these materials and keep track of who has them.

Closing documents. When your investors are ready to write checks or wire money, you'll need legal agreements, like subscription agreements and accredited investor questionnaires. You'll also need to be sure you have the right company structure set up (e.g. a Limited Liability Company, Subchapter S Corporation, C Corporation or Partnership). Free templates are available online, but I recommend finding a good lawyer to guide you through the closing process—one who has a lot of experience working with early-stage companies.

Takeaways

- Use your elevator pitch to identify people interested in learning more about your business (e.g. potential partners, advisors, investors, etc.).
- Send interested parties a one-page synopsis of your business plan, NOT your entire pitch deck. The point is to set up a meeting to deliver your pitch in person for maximum impact.
- If and when it's time to collect checks from investors, hire a startup-oriented lawyer.

Learn more at upstartbootcamp.com

CHAPTER 11

Slide Zero

You've now secured a meeting with your audience—let's say a potential investor. Before you pull out your business plan pitch, you'll have a window of time from when you shake hands with your audience to when you present the first slide in your business plan presentation. I call this window of time "slide zero." Slide zero is something most people forget about, but it can have a significant impact on the outcome of your pitch. Here are two examples from the real world:

- **Allison**. It was one of those mornings for Allison. At 9:00 a.m. she had a pitch in the mid-town office of a leading venture capital firm. At 8:50 a.m. she was still stuck in downtown traffic, thanks to an intense thunderstorm. She arrived late, soaked and frazzled. When the investor came out to meet her, she started a conversation about weather. That conversation continued as they walked down the hall and took their seats in the conference room. Knowing they were behind schedule, Allison jumped right into her pitch. The pitch came off a bit stiff and impersonal, and a day later Allison got an email telling her it was a great idea, but they'd like to see her make more progress on it.[22]

---

22 That means "no" in venture capital-speak.

- **Vincent.** Before his meeting with a potential investor, Vincent did his homework. He learned that the investor had made a previous investment in a company—similar to his—that had failed. He also discovered that he and the potential investor had a mutual friend—a well-respected entrepreneur in a related industry. Vincent arrived early enough to camp out for a coffee nearby and gather his thoughts. When he met his investor in the lobby, he mentioned their mutual contact. The man lit up and told Vincent about a time he had sat on a panel with their mutual friend. Then Vincent mentioned the previous investment and asked what had gone wrong. The investor told him that when the company's customer needs changed, the company's technology took too long and cost too much to modify. Vincent made a mental note to demonstrate the flexibility of his software. He nailed the pitch and landed the investment.

So, what should *you* cover on slide zero?

- **Establish rapport.** If you have a mutual contact that will serve as a confidence-building bridge between you and your audience, mention it. Demonstrate your social skills. Ask an insightful question with a follow-up to show you were listening. See the recommended reading list at the end of this chapter for good tips on how to act, talk, and think when you are in the spotlight.

- **Apply your super-sleuthing skills.** During the banter, try to ferret out a little information that could be helpful to your pitch. Try to find out about experiences or perspectives that could shape the way your audience will react to your material. Are there land mines you should avoid? Hot buttons they'll want you to cover?

Takeaways

- The time during your meeting between when you say "hello" and when you get to your first slide can have a huge impact on your success. I call this "slide zero."
- Use slide zero to establish rapport and to ferret out information you can use to custom-tailor your pitch.

Learn more at upstartbootcamp.com

CHAPTER 12

Pitching Pointers

You used your elevator pitch to gauge the interest of your audience and your one-pager to set up a meeting. You ferreted out some useful information during "slide zero" and now it's time to present your business plan pitch. Here are a few pointers on presenting your pitch:

Cheat. If you've followed my advice, you won't be reading from your slides when you pitch. Instead, you'll use them to keep you on track and to clarify the words you speak. That doesn't mean you have to memorize everything you'll say. Instead, print a copy of your deck and write your name on your copy so you won't accidentally pass it out. Try presenting the deck a few times out loud to yourself and when you hit on wording you like, write notes in the margins. I find those notes helpful on the first pitch or two. After that, I don't need them. It's still nice to have a cheat sheet in case you get nervous or thrown off by tough questions.

Practice. Before you pitch to an investor or advisor, practice on friends and have them do their best to interrupt you, ask you challenging questions, and give you feedback. Develop a list of objections and think through your answers. Look for ways to tweak your deck so you can avoid walking into traps, and begin to build your backup slides.

Prep. Do your homework before you walk into a meeting. Think about what will constitute a "win." Are you looking for a second meeting? An introduction? A verbal commitment? A check? If you don't know what you want, you are less likely to get it. Know your audience. It's easier than ever to do that, thanks to Google, Facebook, LinkedIn, and Twitter, not to mention good old-fashioned networking. Find out about your audience's industry experience, education, and even hobbies. If you are pitching to professional investors, find out what they have invested in, how much they typically invest, at what stage they invest, their industry focus, and any other investment criteria. If possible, find people who have pitched to them (or had them as investors) and get their advice.

Set up. There's nothing more frustrating than having a great presentation ready to go, then running into technical glitches when the meeting starts. Planning to hook up your laptop to a big screen or projector? Find out what equipment will be available and build in extra time to set things up. Bring a backup of your presentation on a memory stick / flash drive and printed copies in case all else fails.

Draw. One approach I find particularly effective is to stop at some point during your presentation and draw a diagram of something on a whiteboard or just a piece of paper. This tends to ramp up the energy level in the meeting and helps to drive a particular point home.

React. Tailor your presentation to your audience and make adjustments as you go. Watch their eyes and body language. Are they sneaking peeks at their BlackBerries, flipping pages, or folding their arms? Pick up the pace. Did they seem to dwell on one of your points or ask an insightful question? Engage them in a dialogue. Provide more detail and ask questions to find out what's on their mind. In fact, try to listen as much as you speak.

Respond. When answering questions, get to the point quickly and be clear and direct. You can add detail as you go if you sense the audience needs more. Be careful not to get defensive or to move beyond your comfort zone. If you really don't know the answer to something, you are usually better off saying you will look into it than taking the chance of flubbing your response.

Tag-team. If you have a business partner, one of you should lead the pitch and the other should provide backup coverage by reading the audience, adding any critical points you've missed, and taking notes on what seems to go well or poorly so you can recap afterward.

 ## Ask the Expert

Frances Cole Jones: "Speak from your own experience, and ask yourself why your audience should care."

Frances Cole Jones is the founder of Cole Media Management, a consultancy that prepares clients for television and print interviews, IPO road shows, and investor pitches. She's also the author of *How to Wow: Proven Strategies for Selling Your (Brilliant) Self in Any Situation*, and *The Wow Factor: The 33 Things You Must (and Must Not) Do to Guarantee Your Edge in Today's Business World*. Jones has prepared clients for appearances on Oprah, Good Morning America, The Today Show, ESPN, Larry King Live, The Discovery Channel, Access Hollywood, E! Entertainment, CNN, and BBC News.

UpStart: "You've advised hundreds of clients on how to make effective presentations. What's the most common mistake you see?"

Frances Cole Jones: "Reading off of their slides. In my dream world I don't want anything on a client's slide coming out of their mouth. We've all been reading since we were about six years old—being read to drives us mad. Slides are meant to enhance talking points, not replace them."

UpStart: "Are there any quick fixes you recommend that can have a big impact?"

Frances Cole Jones: "55 percent of your impact comes from what your body is doing while you are speaking. Only seven percent comes from the words we say. So body language is critical. Keep your hands where people can see them. We trust you when we can see your hands; we don't trust you when we can't. Also, remember the power of storytelling. When you tell a story, filler words like 'um' and 'uh' magically disappear. Speak from your own experience, and ask yourself why your audience should care."

Ask. After your pitch and the ensuing Q&A, ask your audience what they think and whether they are interested in whatever it is you want from them. If you get negative feedback, ask follow-up questions to get to the heart of their concerns. You may not win them over, but you could learn valuable lessons for your next pitch.

Follow-up. Many founders get so caught up in the stress of pitching that they forget simple things like collecting audience contact information and getting everyone present to agree on the next steps.

Finally, keep in mind that your business plan process is iterative. You'll have good pitches and rough ones, but you'll learn from each one. Your pitch will get better and better as you go along and can be a useful tool as a living, breathing roadmap for your company long after you've raised capital or landed a partner.

More resources:

How to Wow: Proven Strategies for Selling Your [Brilliant] Self in Any Situation, by Frances Cole Jones. Jones provides a lot of easy-to-follow tips that can help improve your stage presence and your ability to communicate in a persuasive manner.

Takeaways

- Before you pitch, prepare by creating crib notes and practicing your delivery. Ask questions before you start, to find clues to investor interests.
- During your pitch, react to what investors say—and don't say. Look for opportunities to mix up the pace and energy by drawing on a white board or otherwise stepping away from your slide deck.
- After your pitch, ask for feedback.

Learn more at upstartbootcamp.com

CHAPTER 13

The Fundraising Process

While there are many different approaches to raising capital, there are some industry standards. Companies tend to go through stages of financing. Each stage involves different amounts of capital, types of investors, and uses of proceeds.

	Startup	Seed Round	Series A Round
Source of capital	Your savings Friends and family	Your savings Friends and family Angel investors	Venture Capital
Amount of capital	Typically less than $100K	Up to $1 million	Over $3 million
What you'll do with the money	Conduct research, develop samples/ prototypes	Build core team Launch product Generate revenue	Expand business

Startup Capital. Most entrepreneurs begin with money of their own and money from friends and family. Investors at this stage tend to provide "patient capital"—they'll be happy to make a profit on their investment, but they probably won't be too upset if it takes longer than you expect. These rounds are typically less than $100,000 in total. This startup capital is often used to get a business off the ground by designing a product, creating samples or prototypes, and/or conducting market research. Some companies can get all the way to profitability using startup capital; others must move on to the next stage.

If you raise startup capital from friends and family, you'll have a few ways to structure the deal:

- **Equity capital.** Investors purchase a stake in your company and get a return on their money when you sell the business or go public.

- **Debt.** At this stage it's tough to land a loan from a bank. However, if you need only a small amount of money, like $10,000, you might consider a loan from a family member. To do this, develop a payback schedule and an interest rate (talk to your accountant about this). You should also come up with a contingency plan in case things don't go as intended and you can't pay them back in full, on-time, or at all.

- **Convertible debt.** This is a bit of a hybrid and can work well if you are sure you'll be raising a larger round of financing. For example, I had a client named Paul who had received significant interest from several venture capital firms, but they wanted him to close one big account before stepping up with their investments. He needed $25,000 to cover his costs for the few months he thought it would take to close the account. He also knew that the venture capital firms would be tough negotiators and would probably tell *him* what valuation made sense. So, rather than set a valuation at all, Paul borrowed the money from a friend and structured it as "convertible debt," meaning that when the venture capital money came in, the loan, or debt, would be converted into equity at a discount to the valuation of the VC round. That way, the friend got a good deal and structuring the deal with the VCs was easy.

Food for Thought

Four things you should NOT say to potential investors:

"I really don't want investors meddling in the business." I heard this beauty from someone who asked me for an introduction to an investor. Needless to say, the conversation stopped there.

"Our financial projections are conservative." Puhleeese. You have revenue of, um, zero, now. And within three years you'll have $x0,000,000. Sounds *very* conservative to me.

"I'll send you my pitch deck." NOOOO. Send a one-page synopsis. Present your pitch in person.

"Before I tell you the basic idea, I'll need you to sign an NDA." If you think your basic idea is the true source of the value you'll create over the next three to five years, you have bigger problems. It's (nearly) all about how well you'll execute.

- **Seed Round.** Many companies seek outside[23] financing in order to build a sustainable business. This stage is typically called a "seed stage;" most entrepreneurs get seed-stage capital from angel investors.[24] The investments can be used for many different purposes, but often they are designed to get a company to the point where it has a product or service up and running and enough paying customers to prove that the concept works ("proof of concept").

- **Series A Round.** Companies that need a significant amount of capital after burning through their seed money often seek funding from venture capital firms. For the average entrepreneur, VCs are tough nuts to crack. They tend to invest in a team led by a seasoned entrepreneur with a track

---

23 "Outside" meaning beyond an entrepreneur's capital and that of his/her friends and family.

24 A small number of VCs invest in seed-stage ventures.

record of success and stick to high-growth industries. If you are seeking venture capital, plan on spending six months or more on closing the round, including thorough pre-investment research or "due diligence."[25]

Before approaching any angel, angel group, or venture capital firm, know what type of companies they've invested in previously, and how those companies have performed. Know what type of investment they like to make *now*, which could be different from just a few months ago. Know the background of the key players. And be sure you meet their investment criteria before you waste your time and theirs.

One tactic I've found particularly successful is to start by finding a lead angel—someone with expertise and credibility in your industry. Get that lead to commit before approaching other angels. If the angel is advisory-board worthy (see below), get him/her involved there, too. You can even make the angel's investment contingent upon your ability to raise some minimal amount from others, so the angel's won't be the only money in. Having a lead will give other angels more confidence and will also help settle questions about investment terms.

I did this in the early days of the dot-com boom. Back then (1996), a lot of angel investors wanted to get in on the action they saw around them with companies like Netscape. But things were happening quickly and many angels struggled to make sense of the trends. I had a friend with a high-profile Internet success story and approached him first. He agreed to invest and helped me establish what he thought was a fair valuation for the company, which determined how much of the equity investors would get for their money. Once he committed, I touted him to other prospects as my "lead investor." Other investors trusted his expertise, which lowered their perception of the risk involved.

In general, always seek out "smart money" investors—people with expertise, experience, skills, and the willingness to use them

---

25 Think "proctology exam."

to help grow your business. These investors can provide far more than just a check. They can assist with strategy, provide business development leads, help you find and screen employees, and drum up customers, suppliers, and more. Investors who have been successful entrepreneurs are particularly beneficial. They know what it takes to start a new business and will be useful and understanding.

A few years ago, I started a business with the goal of selling advertisements and promotions on milk containers. The first step was to secure the rights to the space on the milk containers, which are, effectively, little billboards in supermarkets and on kitchen tables. I remember going to my first meeting with a dairy producer and nearly getting laughed out of the room. I'd flown out to a rural Midwestern location for the meeting, wearing a suit that screamed "city slicker." Somehow the dairy guy found out I graduated from Harvard, which was just the ammo he needed to mock me. "I don't know how they do things up at Haaaahvard, but here, we…." Ugh.

Because I had zero experience in the dairy business, I sought out investors with experience in the industry and gave them extra equity options to serve as advisors. One of those investors was a man named Stanley. The next time I went to a dairy meeting, I brought Stanley and I left the suit at home. He spent the first 20 minutes of the meeting shooting the bull with the dairy guy. He found tons of common ground, like conferences they had attended, people they knew, and problems they had faced. He had the right accent, the right look, the right lingo. When it was time to discuss the deal, the dairy guy was open-minded and eager to explore our opportunity.

In addition to finding smart money investors, I often recommend that startups form a board of advisors—not to be confused with a board of directors.[26] Advisors can help entrepreneurs identify

---

26 At startups, the board of directors tends to include founders and significant investors. Directors tend to be formal roles, with voting rights on major decisions and potential liability. Advisors, in contrast,

investors and may invest themselves. They can also help startups in other ways by finding customers, business partners, and employees. To establish an advisory board, start by picking three to five areas where you really need help. Maybe you want a person who has a "golden Rolodex" of industry contacts, another person who is great at sales, and/or a person with expertise in an area where you are weak, like finance or marketing. Then come up with a list of dream advisors in each group, and network your way to them. Make sure each advisor is the kind of person who will enjoy sharing her expertise and helping you build the business from the sidelines as a mentor or coach. Be specific about the role you want him to play, and the amount of time and type of assistance you will want from him. I typically tell advisors I'll need about four hours per month, at their convenience, mostly in the form of phone calls and e-mails. I try to get all the advisors together for lunch or dinner once a quarter. I give each advisor equity options equal to about one percent of the company and vest them over the course of a year or two.

Takeaways

- While there are exceptions, companies tend to go through stages of financing. Each stage involves different amounts of capital, types of investors, and uses of proceeds. Ignoring these norms can be like swimming upstream.
- Always seek out smart money investors—people who can help grow your business, not just write a check.

Learn more at upstartbootcamp.com

---

offer help but don't have voting rights (in their capacity as advisors, anyway).

CHAPTER 14

Valuation

If you are raising capital, be prepared to tell investors your proposed deal terms. Terms can get very complicated, especially with venture capital investors, but I'll stick to the basics in this chapter, since most of you will be raising capital from friends, family, and/or angel investors.

Whether or not to put deal terms in your pitch deck is a matter of style. I often prepare a backup slide with deal terms and pull it out if the pitch is going well or if the investors ask for it. The mechanics are as follows:

1. How much is the company worth today? (pre-money valuation)
2. How much money do you want to raise? (typically enough to get your company through at least 12 months of operations)
3. How much will the company be worth the day after you raise the investment? (AKA post-money valuation)

Let's try some simple round numbers. Say the company is worth $1 million today and you are raising $500,000, so the $1 million it's worth now plus the $500,000 cash from the financing will make the company worth $1.5 million. That means the investors as a group will be putting in $500,000 of the $1.5 million post-money valuation, so they will be buying $500,000/$1,500,000, or 33 percent (a third) of the equity ownership in the company.

Pre-money valuation	$1,000,000	
New investment	$500,000	33%
Post-money valuation	$1,500,000	

The toughest part of this calculation is determining the pre-money valuation. I recently helped a client establish a valuation for his startup. He hadn't raised capital before and his instinct was to value the startup based on projections of future cash flows (a net present value analysis). That can work for a going concern, but startup valuations are typically derived by looking at comparables, meaning recent valuations of other startups being financed.

As I write this, most seed-stage round valuations tend to range from $500,000 to $2 million. Factors that determine where a startup falls along this spectrum include:

- **Quality of the team.** Have they founded successful businesses before and made money for investors?

- **Stage of development.** Is this an entrepreneur with a business plan and nothing more? Does she have a prototype developed? Paying customers?

- **Size of the opportunity.** Is this a company that could, in theory, become a $10 million business or does it have the potential to be a $100 million business?

- **Sweat equity implications.** If the valuation is too low in relation to the amount raised, the management team may own a very small stake. That's bad for you as an entrepreneur, because you won't have enough incentive to make the sacrifices necessary to build the company. It's also bad for investors; they want you motivated to work hard to make the company valuable, so you all make money when the company is sold.

After considering these issues, my client and I came up with a target pre-money valuation. Our number was $1.5 million. His goal was to raise $500,000, so he'd be selling $500,000/($1,500,000 + $500,000), or 25 percent of his equity, to the new investors.

Like any good entrepreneur, he was concerned about giving away too much equity and thought he should try for a $3 million pre-money valuation. It took a bit of discussion, but I convinced him otherwise. Of course, I want the best for my clients, but if he walked into a meeting with a sophisticated investor with a valuation that's out of line with what's happening in the market, he could lose credibility and blow the deal. If he were to convince an unsophisticated investor (say, a family member) to take the higher valuation, he could have a different problem: down the road, if he took money from a venture capital firm, they might strike a tougher bargain, in which case the unsophisticated investor might suffer significant dilution.

Many entrepreneurs and investors agonize over valuations. After all, valuations impact how much each party earns if the company is acquired or goes public. But some take it too far. I recently read an insightful blog entry by Paul Graham, successful entrepreneur and founder of business incubator Y Combinator:

> "There is no rational way to value an early-stage startup. The valuation reflects nothing more than the strength of the company's bargaining position... Ultimately it doesn't matter much. When angels make a lot of money from a deal, it's not because they invested at a valuation of $1.5 million instead of $3 million. It's because the company was really successful. I can't emphasize that too much. Don't get hung up on mechanics or deal terms. What you should spend your time thinking about is whether the company is good. Similarly, founders also should not get hung up on deal terms, but should spend their time thinking about how to make the company good."[27]

---

27 http://www.paulgraham.com/angelinvesting.html#f1n

Takeaways

- Valuation of early-stage ventures is more of an art than a science.
- The exercise involves making a case for what the company is worth today (pre-money valuation), stating how much it will raise from investors, and calculating resulting ownership percentages.

Learn more at upstartbootcamp.com

CHAPTER 15

Off To The Races

Writing a business plan, raising capital, and launching a new business are no easy feats. They demand guts, perseverance, and resourcefulness, among other things. And yet, these steps merely get you to the starting line. The real value creation is just beginning.

As a fellow entrepreneur, I'm well aware of the daunting challenges that await you. Still, I'd rather encourage you to follow your dreams than dissuade you from trying. Building a new, successful company is one of the most rewarding business experiences possible.

Finally, a few last words of advice to consider as you set out on your adventure:

- **Stay focused.** Great entrepreneurs know what they're going after and don't let anything get in the way—including tangential opportunities that are best left to be done down the line. Keep your strategy and tactics simple and get the execution right. Hit your initial milestones before you branch out into new territory.

- **Get help.** It takes a village to build a company. You can't do it alone. Enlist the support of your investors, advisors, partners, family, and friends. These people make up your extended team. This is no time to be proud. Be aware of your weaknesses, and shore them up by getting help.

- **Stop and reflect.** Building a company is a bit like swimming underwater. You set your sights, dive down, and swim all-out and as long as you can hold your breath. But you have to surface periodically to breathe and get your bearings. With a startup, you have to stop swimming once in a while. You'll need to see what's going on in the world around you, make sure you are still swimming in the right direction, and take stock of your accomplishments as well as the challenges ahead.

- **Track progress.** Set quantitative goals for the business, make your extended team aware of them, and measure your results against your goals. It will help you stay objective and give you added encouragement to produce results.

- **Adjust strategy.** Chances are, the first strategy you follow won't be the one that ultimately prevails. The trick is to stick with good ideas long enough to see if they can work, but be ready to let go of them before it's too late. How do you know when it's time? Use progress against your goals as a measurement and your extended team as judges.

David Ronick

David Ronick is a serial entrepreneur and founder of UpStart Bootcamp, an online school for startups. UpStart Bootcamp emphasizes the importance of speed, flexibility, and capital efficiency and offers startups inspiration, knowledge, and access to people who can help.

Ronick has provided consulting services to hundreds of startups, including those planned by Mark Gordon (producer), Moby (recording artist), Pat McGrath (makeup artist), and Tiki Barber (athlete, journalist). He has also advised dozens of brands on new initiatives, including Pampers, BlackBerry, and Rolling Stone.

Ronick's own startups include one of the first social networks, a provider of online software for human resources, and a company that runs promotions on the packages of consumer products.

Ronick judges business plan contests for schools, including The Harvard Business School, and is a frequent speaker on new venture creation. Ronick is a graduate of The Harvard Business School and of Brown University. He lives in Greenwich Village, New York, with his wife and son.

Glossary

- Advisory board – a group of people that provide strategic and operating advice to a startup. This group is less formal and has less legal accountability than a board of directors.

- Angel investor – an individual who invests his/her own money in startups.

- Angel network – a group of angel investors that review opportunities together.

- Back-of-the-envelope calculations – simple calculations, such as ratios, that can provide useful analysis.

- Bootstrapping – pulling yourself up by your bootstraps, or launching a startup with minimal outside financing.

- Bottom-up planning – conducting forecasts by starting with small increments, like weekly or monthly activities.

- Break-even volume – the number of units a company must sell in order to break even or have unit contribution cover overhead.

- Burn rate – the amount of cash an unprofitable company loses each month.

- Business model – the way a company generates revenue and the degree to which each transaction or sale contributes to profits.

- Communities of interest – groups of people already assembled, with similar needs or behaviors.

- Convertible debt – a type of loan that can be exchanged for ownership or equity.

- Customer acquisition cost – the expenses associated with attracting one incremental customer.

- Dilution – the degree to which a shareholder's ownership percentage is reduced by future issues of equity, such as when a company sells more stock or grants stock to employees.

- Due diligence – the process by which investors research potential investments.

- Elevator pitch – a very short explanation of what a company does and why it's positioned for success.

- Exit strategy – a plan for providing liquid returns to investors, often consisting of selling the company (i.e. having it acquired or taking it public in an initial public offering ("IPO").

- Friends and family round – investments provided by a founder's own friends and family members (sometimes "fools" is added to this term, implying that early-stage investors take unwise risks).

- Hockey stick – when the graph of a company's protected financial performance makes a sudden and sharp spike for the better, in the shape of a hockey stick.

- Lead investor – the first person to commit capital to a round of financing, ideally acting as a bellwether for other investors.

- Lifetime value per customer – the amount of margin an incremental customer provides over the entire course of his/her relationship with a company.

- Liquidity event – an event that provides liquid returns to investors, often consisting of a sale of the company or an initial public offering ("IPO").

- Non-disclosure agreement ("NDA") – an agreement that limits one or more parties from sharing sensitive information related to a startup or other entity.

- Overhead – fixed costs that don't vary directly with sales volume, such as rent, staffing, and utilities.

- Pitch deck – a presentation designed to influence an audience, often made with software such as PowerPoint or Keynote.

- Proof of concept – establishing evidence that a company has viability, often consisting of positive sales results.

- Profit margin – profits divided by revenue.

- Pyramid of influence – the process by which the behavior of certain groups or tiers of customers impacts other groups, such as when consumers emulate celebrities.

- Seed capital – an early round of financing, often provided by founders, friends and family members, and/or angel investors.

- Smart money – investors who bring more to a startup than capital, such as advice and introductions to customers, suppliers, partners or employees.

- Solopreneur – an entrepreneur building a one-person startup.

- Substitution – a product or service that customers may use in lieu of another type of product or service, such as using olive oil for cooking instead of butter.

- Sweat equity – capital a founder earns through his or her own hard work and generation of results.

- Total addressable market – the revenue opportunity available for a specific type of product or service within a particular market.

- Traction – progress toward goals, such as building a team, developing a product, closing distribution deals, or selling to customers.

- Unit contribution – the amount of margin generated by one transaction or sale.

- Unit economics – analysis of the revenues and costs generated by one transaction or sale.

- Valuation – the amount of money a company is worth, which can be a tricky calculation for a startup.

- Variable costs – costs that vary directly with the number of units sold, such as sales commissions or the cost of manufacturing (AKA "cost of goods sold").

- Venture capitalist – people who invest in early-stage companies on behalf of a fund.

- Vesting – a process of transferring ownership. For example, many companies grant equity to employees, but those employees take ownership of this equity over time, following a schedule meant to keep them working at the company long enough to help generate sufficient value to earn that equity.

CPSIA information can be obtained at www.ICGtesting.com
Printed in the USA
268429BV00004B/95/P